THE AMERICAN
ACCOUNTANTS' MANUAL

THE DEVELOPMENT OF CONTEMPORARY ACCOUNTING THOUGHT

Advisory Editor
Richard P. Brief

Editorial Board
Gary John Previts
Basil S. Yamey
Stephen A. Zeff

THE
AMERICAN ACCOUNTANTS' MANUAL

FRANK BROAKER

AND

RICHARD M. CHAPMAN

ARNO PRESS
A New York Times Company
New York • 1978

Editorial Supervision: LUCILLE MAIORCA

———◆———

Reprint Edition 1978 by Arno Press Inc.

THE DEVELOPMENT OF CONTEMPORARY ACCOUNTING THOUGHT
ISBN for complete set: 0-405-10891-5
See last pages of this volume for titles.

Manufactured in the United States of America

———◆———

Library of Congress Cataloging in Publication Data

Broaker, Frank.
    The American accountants' manual.

    (The Development of contemporary accounting
thought)
    Reprint of the ed. published by Broaker &
Chapman, New York.
    Includes index.
    1. Accounting--Examination, questions, etc.
I. Chapman, Richard Marvin, joint author.
II. Title. III. Series.
HF5661.B7 1978   657'.076   77-87264
ISBN 0-405-10893-1

THE
AMERICAN ACCOUNTANTS' MANUAL

VOLUME I.

EXAMINATION QUESTIONS

PREPARED BY THE STATE BOARD OF EXAMINERS OF EXPERT PUBLIC ACCOUNTANTS
APPOINTED BY THE BOARD OF REGENTS OF THE UNIVERSITY OF THE STATE
OF NEW YORK, PURSUANT TO CHAPTER 312, LAWS OF 1896, ENTITLED
"AN ACT TO REGULATE THE PROFESSION OF PUBLIC ACCOUNTANTS."

First licensing examination for the issue of certificates to "Certified Public Accountants" conferring the right
to use the distinguishing initials C. P. A., held at Buffalo and New York, Tuesday and Wednesday, December
15th and 16th, 1896.

SUBJECTS: THEORY OF ACCOUNTS; PRACTICAL ACCOUNTING;
AUDITING; COMMERCIAL LAW.

TOGETHER WITH

ANSWERS

IN CONCISE FORM, FURTHER ELUCIDATED BY AUTHOR'S COMMENTARIES UPON THE TECHNIQUE
AND EXPRESSION OF MODERN ACCOUNTANCY.

Especially designed as a manual for accountants and students.
Imparting the higher logical and scientific conception of the subject now recognized to be above and supplementary
to Counting House Book-keeping.

BY

FRANK BROAKER, C. P. A.,
STATE EXAMINER OF PUBLIC ACCOUNTANTS
—AND—
PRESIDENT AMERICAN ASSOCIATION OF PUBLIC ACCOUNTANTS.

Assisted by his business partner,
RICHARD M. CHAPMAN, C. P. A.,

PUBLISHED BY
BROAKER & CHAPMAN.
CERTIFIED PUBLIC ACCOUNTANTS,
(AMERICAN TRACT SOCIETY BUILDING.)
150 NASSAU STREET,
NEW YORK.

C. W. GAUDINEER, PRINTER AND BOOK BINDER, NEW YORK

CERTIFIED PUBLIC ACCOUNTANTS.

Laws of New York, 1896, ch. 312.

AN ACT TO REGULATE THE PROFESSION OF PUBLIC ACCOUNTANTS.

§ 1.   Any citizen of the United States, or person who has duly declared his intention of becoming such citizen, residing or having a place for the regular transaction of business in the state, being over the age of 21 years and of good moral character, and who shall have received from the regents of the University a certificate of his qualifications to practise as a public expert accountant as hereinafter provided, shall be styled and known as a certified public accountant; and no other person shall assume such title, or use the abbreviation C. P. A. or any other words, letters or figures, to indicate that the person using the same is such certified public accountant.

§ 2.   The regents of the University shall make rules for the examination of persons applying for certificates under this act, and may appoint a board of three examiners for the purpose, which board shall, after the year 1897, be composed of certified public accountants. The regents shall charge for examination and certificate such fee as may be necessary to meet the actual expenses of such examinations, and they shall report, annually, their receipts and expenses under the provisions of this act to the state comptroller, and pay the balance of receipts over expenditures to the state treasurer.   The regents may revoke any such certificate for sufficient cause after written notice to the holder thereof and a hearing thereon.

§ 3.   The regents may, in their discretion, waive the examination of any person possessing the qualifications mentioned in § 1 who shall have been, for more than one year before the passage of this act, practising in the state on his own account, as a public accountant, and who shall apply in writing for such certificate within one year after the passage of this act.

§ 4.   Any violation of this act shall be a misdemeanor.

§ 5.   This act shall take effect immediately.

Notes on the Law.

1   The use of the abbreviation C. P. A. or any other words, letters or figures to indicate that the person using the same is a certified public accountant is prohibited except to those holding regents' certificates.

2   The three examiners are to be appointed to serve for one, two and three years respectively. After 1897 the board is to be composed of certified public accountants.

3   Certificates will be revoked for cause.

4   Examinations may be waived on unanimous recommendation of the examiners in the case of candidates well known to them as meeting the professional requirements and as having been in reputable practice as public accountants since Jan. 1, 1890, the same fee to be paid as for examination.

5   The full C. P. A. certificate is to be granted only to those at least 25 years of age who have had five years' satisfactory experience in the study or practice of accounting.

6   Candidates having the required preliminary education and passing the required examinations, but lacking the age or the five years' experience required for the full C. P. A. certificate may be certified as junior accountants under the same conditions as to residence and character.

7.   Two examinations, in June and in December, are to be held annually.   There are to be four sessions of three hours each as follows: 1 Theory of accounts.   2 Practical accounting.   3 Auditing. 4 Commercial law.

8.   Candidates must complete all four subjects at a single examination as required in medicine.

9   Candidates for either the C. P. A. or the junior accountant certificate must be more than 21 years of age and of good moral character.   They must pay a fee of $25, and must have the regents' academic diploma or its equivalent as prescribed for other professional examinations.

10   The regents will accept as fully equivalent to the academic diploma any one of the following:

a   A certificate of having successfully completed at least one full year's course of study in the collegiate department of any college or university, registered by the regents as maintaining a satisfactory standard.

b   A certificate of having passed in a registered institution examinations equivalent to the full collegiate course of the freshman year or to a completed academic course.

Three full academic years of satisfactory work may be accepted as a high school course till Aug. 1, 1896, when four full academic years will be required.

c   Regent's passcards for any 48 academic counts or any regent's diploma.

d   A certificate of graduation from any registered gymnasium in Germany, Austria or Russia.

e   A certificate of the successful completion of a course of five years in a registered Italian *gimnasio* and three years in a *liceo*.

f   The bachelor's degree in arts or science, or substantial equivalents from any registered institution in France or Spain.

g   Any credential from a registered institution or from the government in any state or country which represents the completion of a course of study equivalent to graduation from a registered New York high school or academy or from a registered Prussian gymnasium.

The first examination under this law is to be held in New York city and in Buffalo Tuesday and Wednesday, December 15 and 16, 1896; the second in New York city, Albany, Syracuse and Buffalo, Tuesday and Wednesday, June 15 and 16, 1897.   Application should be made at least 10 days in advance to Examination department, University of the State of New York, Albany, N. Y.

PREFACE.

The legal recognition of accountancy as a learned profession and the enactment of a law to regulate this profession being accomplished facts, and examinations having been held by the Regents of the University of the State of New York upon technical papers prepared by a board of examiners duly appointed by them and composed of professional practicing accountants, it becomes obviously proper and imperative that immediate attention should be directed to the creation and establishment of technical literature, of a standard that will recommend its adoption as authentic and contribute to the building up of a curriculum for accountant students who may seek to qualify themselves to enter the accountancy profession and thereafter practice as Certified Public Accountants.

The best subjects that present themselves and call for promptest treatment are those contained in or suggested by the first examination questions, which were prepared with extreme care to indicate the lines upon which future accountancy examinations would be continued, and while succeeding examinations will treat more minutely with special subjects, great importance is attached to these initial questions as affording a general finger post to the avenues of study into which accountant students' attention should be first directed.

In formulating each answer no digression from the subject matter of the immediate question has been made, but in order to render it instructive, self-explanatory and cause it to support without repeating kindred principles presented in other questions, its treatment has been more extended and comprehensive than would be practicable within the time afforded by candidates undergoing examination, whose answers would have for their main purpose, more the determining of their acquaintance with the subject than a didactic elucidation of it.

The technique and expression of modern accountancy respecting which there has been keenly felt a want of literature of a character sufficiently speculative, logical and meritorious to be in keeping with the accountancy profession as recently dignified by legislative enactment, and entering upon a course fraught with powers of usefulness and importance scarcely to be estimated, renders it at once incumbent upon those entrusted with its destiny to labor assiduously in this field and bring about a much needed uniformity in practice.

THE AUTHORS.

TABLE OF CONTENTS.

THEORY OF ACCOUNTS.

THEORY OF ACCOUNTS.

Q. 1. State the essential principles of double entry book-keeping, and show wherein it differs from single entry book-keeping.

A. 1. The essential principles of double entry bookkeeping are :

First. That every transaction is a transfer of money or of money's worth, that it therefore involves a giver and a receiver; consequently requiring an entry to be made both in the account which is diminished and in the account which is increased.

Second. What is parted with is deducted from the account which is diminished by it and from which it is taken, by posting the item to the right hand or credit side of such account, and what is received in exchange is added to the account which is increased by it and to which it is given, by posting the item to the left hand or debit side of such account, thereby establishing an equilibrium between debits and credits and thus affording a proof that every transaction has been posted correctly as to amounts.

Third. Double entry bookkeeping thus provides for the maintenance of accounts so relating the one to the other, that while one class of accounts will collectively show the assets and liabilities, the other class will show the profits and losses, and both classes equally display and confirm the resultant surplus or deficit.

Single entry implies no particular application or limitation of system, but in so far as it may be regarded as a system it deals simply with details and forms of entries for the purpose of recording charges to customers and obligations to creditors, and while personal book accounts are maintained in the same form as in double entry, the complementary accounts relating to revenue are omitted and the element of equilibrium or balance between debits and credits pervading double entry is not established.

In the absence of the confirmatory scheme of revenue accounts peculiar to double entry, the profits or losses in single entry are periodically ascertained by a comparison between past and present condition, the property values are arrived at by appraisement and stock taking and the accuracy of final results are susceptible of no other proof than a careful detailed review would afford.

Q. 2. Describe the following and show wherein they differ:

(a) Trial Balance.

(b) Balance Sheet.

(c) Statement of Affairs.

(d) Realization and Liquidation Account.

A. 2. (a) A Trial Balance is a list or schedule of the accounts in the ledger or ledgers of a business remaining open, as at the end of a day specified, showing the ledger folio, name, and Dr. or Cr. balance or Dr. and Cr. footings of each account in turn, and showing an equal aggregate sum of debits and credits. The purpose of a trial balance is primarily to test and demonstrate the equilibrium of the ledger, which, although not proving the absolute correctness of the ledger in all respects, is nevertheless essential to such correctness, and is a preliminary process to closing the books and preparing the business and financial statements.

(b) A Balance Sheet is a statement of the assets and liabilities of a business, as at the end of a day specified, and is generally prepared after closing the books at the end of a fiscal period, to ascertain and show the financial condition of the business at the time. It is compiled from the trial balance by bringing together and arranging only such accounts as represent assets and liabilities, supplemented by inventories, reserves, unexpired charges, unmatured obligations, and sundry items disclosed by adjustment; the remaining accounts upon the trial balance, generally designated as "nominal accounts", are simultaneously closed and carried to a general profit and loss account in the ledger, and collectively form the subject of the profit and loss statement that usually accompanies the balance sheet. The open book accounts of trade debtors and creditors appear upon the balance sheet in two aggregate amounts, and are either supported by schedules, or reference is made to the page of trial balance book whereon the respective totals appear. A balance sheet therefore contains the same accounts that appear on the trial balance at the commencement of the next fiscal period after the nominal accounts have all been closed, but further classified and arranged so as to give the clearest possible expression to the results.

(c) A Statement of Affairs is a summary of the schedules of liabilities and assets of an insolvent debtor, so arranged as to show both actual and contingent liabilities and to what extent the same are secured; also to show both the nominal or book value of the assets and what they are expected to produce. It is prepared for the purpose of ascertaining and indicating the true condition of the estate with reference to realization, and the extent of the deficiency with respect to liquidation. The creditors are classified in separate schedules as, unsecured, partially secured, fully secured, contingent and preferential, the latter schedule being deducted directly from the assets. The assets, as to properties, are arranged in the order of prospective realization, and probable shrinkage is indicated, and as to book debtors, are classified in separate schedules as, good, doubtful and bad. It is frequently accompanied by a "deficiency account" which, starting at the commencement of the business, or, if impracticable, at the last date of solvency, recites the capital invested by the insolvent debtor, the amounts withdrawn for personal expenses, the business losses subsequently sustained and the shrinkages in prospective realization, which collectively account for the deficiency by which the Statement of Affairs is balanced.

(d) A Realization and Liquidation Account is a statement prepared for the purpose of showing the results of the winding up or closing out of a business or estate. It is first charged with the total assets and credited with the total liabilities exclusive of capital; it is next credited with the net proceeds realized from the assets and charged with the total expenditure in liquidating the liabilities together with the costs of realization; the balance, being a profit or loss incidental to the winding up, is carried to capital. When the winding up is undertaken by a trustee, his account is charged with the amount realized from assets and credited with the payment of liabilities, together with costs and expenses, and the balance of his account when handed over is carried to capital account and balances and closes the same.

A Trial Balance is, therefore, the main source from which the material for the succeeding forms of statements are procured, and differs from them, as they differ from each other, in the form that it assumes and the specific purpose for which it is intended. Whereas a Trial Balance establishes little else than the equilibrium of the ledger, a Balance Sheet arranges the items into a financial statement, from which in cases of insolvency a Statement of Affairs is framed, or provides the first basis for a Realization and Liquidation Account upon the final winding up.

Q. 3.   In devising a system of accounts for a business, what are the main subjects for consideration, and in what order should they have attention?

A. 3.   The main subjects for consideration in devising a system of accounts are :

First—To ascertain the character of the assets and liabilities, to determine their order of classification and to what extent they may with advantage be contained in separate accounts, to the end of arriving at a permanent form in which the balance sheet may be clearly expressed.

Second—To ascertain the sources of income and profits, and of the expenses and losses incidental to the business, having regard to the characteristic elements of cost, proceeds, fixed charges, management expenses, maintenance, depreciation, reserves, and all other classes of income and expenditure necessary to a comprehensive and intelligible statement of revenue.

Third—To design books of original entry, with suitable arrangement of columns to receive and allocate the various items in such manner as to afford data leading up to the balance sheet and revenue account as formulated, and directly contributing to the aggregate items appearing thereon.

Fourth—To institute suitable procedure and organization in the methods of treating with details and bringing the transactions upon the books, with a view to economy of time, accuracy of work, and facility of agreeing and balancing the accounts to the furthest possible subdivision.

Fifth—To render the system susceptible of a thorough and rapid audit, and capable of readily making apparent any irregularity arising from ignorance, stupidity or dishonesty.

Q. 4. Describe the following and show wherein they differ:

(a) Revenue Account.

(b) Trading Account.

(c) Profit and Loss Account.

(d) Deficiency Account.

A. 4. (a) A Revenue Account is the comprehensive title of all accounts treating in detail or summary with the subjects of income, earnings or profits, and against such the cost, expenses or losses incident thereto, the former subjects being credits and the latter charges to Revenue. In non-trading concerns, namely those simply administering funds, the revenue account is either stated under that title or styled "Income and Expenditure Account", whereas in trading concerns engaged in manufacturing, buying and selling commodities, the title "Profit and Loss Account" is nearly always used, and is frequently divided into two sections designated respectively "Trading Account" and "Profit and Loss Account."

(b) A Trading Account deals with the subjects of cost and proceeds. Cost comprises outlay for materials, freight, duty and other charges incidental to acquiring possession, as also labor bestowed in manufacturing or rendering the wares salable. and constitutes charges to the account. Proceeds comprise returns in the form of sales or other equivalent and constitute credits to the account. The inventories of stock at the beginning and end of the period covered by the account, being also charged and credited respectively (the credit being usually effected, in the preparation of a statement, by deduction from the charges instead of credit entry, in order that the sales may rank alone as proceeds and the net cost appear as an offset), the balance of the account usually designated as "Gross Profits" is carried to Profit and Loss Account.

(c) A Profit and Loss Account, when constituting the second section of the revenue account, is credited with the gross profit from the trading account together with whatever other sources of income may contribute to the profits of the business; and is charged with the management expenses incident to the general conduct of the business, as for instance, rent, insurance, interest, salaries of clerks, advertising, office supplies, etc.; the final balance designated "Net Profits" or "Net Losses" is either carried to capital, as in the case of a single proprietorship or a partnership, or left standing as undivided surplus to the credit of profit and loss on the books of a corporation, subject to dividends or other disposition. It is often found expedient to append a third revenue section for dealing with extraordinary profits or losses, which, while affecting the surplus, are foreign to the legitimate or normal transactions of the business, in which case the balance brought down from the second section is further qualified and distinguished as "Net Profit on Trading" or "Net Loss on Trading" and the final balance of profit or loss is stated simply as "Net Profit" or "Net Loss." The Trading Account as a separate statement or section of the revenue is frequently dispensed with, and the Profit and Loss Account is made to comprehend the entire subject, in which case the distinction between "gross profits" and "net profits" is not marked.

(d) A Deficiency Account is designed to accompany the statement of affairs of an insolvent debtor's estate. It is charged with the deficiency as shown by the statement of affairs, capital invested at commencement of period under review and any profit extraordinary to the general trading. It is credited with losses and shrinkages in values as exhibited by the statement of affairs, liability upon endorsement of notes other than debtor's own acceptances, in the amount anticipated to rank for dividends, loss on trading and drawings from business for private use. A deficiency account is therefore a summary, accounting for the deficiency appearing upon the statement of affairs, and displays in classified form the causes that have contributed to the failure, in so far as they relate to the revenue and the extinction of capital, and affords the basis for a critical inquiry for judging of the honest misfortune or premeditated designs of the insolvent debtor.

Q. 5. State the purposes for which series of perpendicular columns are employed in books of original entry and how these purposes may be accomplished relative to the following conditions:

(a) Several ledgers comprehended in one system of accounts.

(b) Several departments comprehended in one business.

(c) Several accounts comprehended in income and expenditure.

A. 5. The primitive application of the principle of double entry necessitated the actual as well as the theoretical posting of each and every entry separately to the accounts respectively debited and credited therewith, but later modifications of the actual practice have demonstrated that (without any departure from the principle "for every debit there must be a credit") in so far as either side of the entries are required to be posted to nominal accounts, or accounts representing other than customers or creditors in %c with the business, said sides of the entries could be allocated in the books of original entry under the headings of the nominal or business accounts affected, by distributing them throughout a series of columns provided for that purpose, and instead of the detailed posting of every separate item to said nominal accounts, only the daily, weekly or monthly footings of the columns need be posted to accomplish the same purpose and end.

(a) When the ledger is divided into several sections or comprehends several separate volumes, each alloted to a different class of accounts, the items on the books of original entry may be correspondingly classified by providing therein separate columns for the items that are to be posted to each of the separate ledgers or ledger sections mentioned, and although there may be some books of original entry exclusively appertaining to distinct sections of the ledger, the general cash book and other books of a comprehensive nature will require to be columnized according to the ledgers with which they articulate, in order that the aggregate totals of debits and credits in each ledger and its collective balance may be readily ascertained, by bringing together and summarizing the totals of the various columns in the books of original entry appertaining thereto.

(b) Where several departments are separately maintained in the accounts, the sales book, instead of showing one general credit of proceeds, may be divided into departmental columns for collecting and totaling the items of proceeds arising from each separate department. In like manner the invoice or purchase book, in so far as it relates to cost or direct departmental charges, instead of showing one collective charge to trading, will be provided with columns for collecting and totaling the expenditure against each department. The same distinction may be made in all other transactions affecting the several departments, whether constituting cancellation of items coming through the returns and allowance book, or direct cash expenditure appearing in the cash or petty cash book, and where the frequency of the items renders it expedient, a corresponding system of columns may also be maintained.

(c) The nominal accounts dealing with general income and expenditure are also made the subjects of separate columns in the books of original entry on which the several items appear, those relating to general management expenses, when the same give rise to liabilities subsequently liquidated, frequently form an additional system of columns in the invoice or purchase book, supplementary to the trade charges, and together with the latter form the aggregate debit, complementary to the credits in the sundry personal accounts.

The employment of systems of columns not only reduces the volume of posting from separate items to total sums, but affords a valuable check upon the additions, by agreement between the footings of the opposing columns, and practically balances and verifies much of the work, before the postings to the ledger are made.

Q. 6. Describe the following and show wherein they differ :

(a) Statement of Income and Expenditure.

(b) Statement of Receipts and Payments.

A. 6. (a) An Income and Expenditure Account (like a profit and loss account) states the entire income for the period to which it relates without regard to whether the same has been collected or received in cash ; and also the total expenses properly chargeable against said income without regard to whether the same have been paid or are still owing, and therefore takes cognizance of outstanding assets and liabilities both at the commencement and close of said period. The final balance of income and expenditure represents the surplus of income over expenditure or vice versa, either for the period under review or including the balance brought forward from the previous account.

(b) A Statement of Receipts and Payments is a summarized cash account and states the amount of money actually received and disbursed during the period to which it relates without regard to whether the same are earnings or expenses exclusively appertaining to that period or include items so appertaining to the period preceding. It starts with the cash balance at the commencement of the period which it covers and concludes with the cash balance at the close thereof.

If, therefore, the assets and liabilities outstanding at the commencement of the period and since settled, be deducted from the receipts and payments respectively, and those since contracted and outstanding at the close of the period be added thereto, the final balance thereof will agree with the income and expenditure account for the same period. An Income and Expenditure Account verifies the surplus appearing upon the balance sheet which it usually accompanies. A Statement of Receipts and Payments verifies the asset of cash appearing upon the balance sheet, and is usually the subject of a Treasurer's report.

Q. 7. Describe a method of keeping accounts so that the aggregate sums due from customers and due to creditors can be known without preparing a schedule of the accounts of such customers and creditors, and so that an independent balance of the ledger, containing only the real, nominal, special and controlling accounts, exclusive of the individual accounts of customers and trade creditors may be taken.

A. 7.   This method necessitates the division of the ledger into three distinct sections, viz :

First—Customers' Ledger, containing the individual accounts of customers or trade debtors.

Second—Creditors' Ledger, containing the individual accounts of trade creditors.

Third—Nominal Ledger, containing all other accounts, i. e., real, nominal, special and controlling accounts.

For illustration, we will ideally regard the customers collectively, as one person, and the creditors collectively as one person, and open two summary accounts, one for each, in the Nominal Ledger, under the respective headings :

"Sundry Customers" controlling account.

"Sundry Creditors" controlling account.

By collecting in separate columns, provided therefor in the books of original entry, all the debit and credit items that are to be posted to the Customers' Ledger and the Creditors' Ledger, and posting the totals of said columns to their respective controlling accounts in the Nominal Ledger, the Nominal Ledger will balance independently of the other ledgers, and the balances of the controlling accounts will equal the aggregate sum of the balances of the open individual accounts in the ledgers they respectively represent and control.

When the distinction between customers and creditors is not practicable, for the reason that purchases from and sales to the same persons are extensively made, the customers' and creditors' ledgers may be combined and controlled by one summary account headed "Sundry Trade Debtors and Creditors."

The foregoing method renders it practicable to balance and close the Nominal Ledger as soon as the entries in the books of original entry are completed and the comparatively few postings to the Nominal Ledger are made, and before the more numerous postings to the debtors' and creditors' accounts are completed and the lengthy schedules of balances are taken off and agreed. The Nominal Ledger not only shows in advance the correct balances that the debtors' and creditors' ledgers must show when completed, but furnishes absolute assurance of their accuracy when determined by the balances of the aggregate values contained in the controlling accounts as verified by the equilibrium of the Nominal Ledger.

Q. 8. Define and differentiate :

(a) Capital and Revenue.

(b) Capital Receipts and Revenue Receipts.

(c) Capital Expenditure and Revenue Expenditure.

A. 8. (a) The term "Capital" as used in accounts, while invariably conveying the one fundamental idea has, however, many shadings of significance, arising from the various relationships its radical principle sustains to the many laws and themes of accountancy.

Capital is the surplus of assets over liabilities, and is the indebtedness of a business to its proprietor or proprietors for unimpaired investment and accumulated profits, and in this sense is the antithesis to "Deficit", which latter is the surplus of liabilities over assets, and is the indebtedness of the proprietor or proprietors to the business for losses sustained in excess of the extinction of the original investment. Capital therefore comprehends any and all properties and assets employed in a business, as the positive element, and all liabilities and obligations owing or extant, as the negative element, and in this sense is the antithesis to "Revenue", which latter comprehends the profits or losses resulting from the business transactions.

Revenue is the amount earned by the carrying on of an undertaking, and is the excess of the profits and income, over the expenses and losses incidental thereto. If the expenses and losses exceed the profits and income, there is no revenue, and capital is accordingly decreased by either the depletion of accumulated surplus, or the impairment of the original investment, which is sometimes termed a "revenue loss", the word "revenue" being used in its generic sense as relating only to the elements, which normally would have created it.

(b) Receipts, unless specifically qualified, are generally understood to mean receipts of cash. The term "Capital Receipts" would therefore imply the cash received from stockholders in a corporation upon the payment of their subscriptions to the capital stock. But the practice of issuing stock for property purchased without any cash transaction has become such an established custom, that any species of receipts may be represented and the capital stock account be designated upon the balance sheet as "Capital Receipts" for the full amount issued. A funded debt upon the properties of a corporation, creating a bond and mortgage account upon the books, also frequently appears upon the balance sheet under the heading "capital receipts"; the capital stock and funded debt being then distinguished by the sub-headings of "share capital" and "loan capital" respectively.

Although the term "capital receipts" generally appears upon the balance sheet of a corporation, it is frequently used in speaking of any capital investment, whether in a corporation or otherwise, and has a further significance as being the proceeds from the sale of a fixed property or capital asset as distinguished from the sale of the wares which it may be the business of the concern to dispose of in the regular course of trade.

Revenue Receipts differ from capital receipts in being the income derived from the earnings of capital invested (and includes no part of the principal) or the proceeds arising from the trading transactions in so far as they constitute profits to the business.

(c) The term "Expenditure" signifies not only the payment or disbursement of cash, but also the exchange of any other property or the creation of any debt or liability as the consideration for property acquired, services received, or means and facilities attained.

Capital Expenditure is the exchange of one property for another, and being merely permutative in character results in neither an increase or decrease of capital; as for instance, the purchase of real estate, machinery or merchandise, so far as it involves the payment of money or creation of liability is an expenditure, but as equivalent value is acquired and the capital is undisturbed it is designated "capital expenditure". In a more restricted sense the term denotes the expenditure by a corporation of its capital receipts and accumulated surplus, in acquiring or extending its plant and other assets of a permanent nature.

Revenue Expenditure comprises all that class of expenditures, modificative in character, which result in a decrease of capital as against the increase thereof resulting from revenue receipts. It includes all charges against the income and profits; those constituting direct business expenses as rents, rates and taxes, insurance, salaries, commissions, advertising, etc., the maintenance and repairs of fixed properties, as well as depreciation, bad accounts and all business losses.

Capital and revenue expenditures are frequently alluded to as "charges to capital" and "charges to revenue" respectively, and correspondingly capital and revenue receipts are respectively distinguished by the terms "credits to capital" and "credits to revenue."

Q. 9.   How may the accounts in a trial balance be best arranged to facilitate the preparation of a business and financial statement?

A. 9.   In the absence of a clear conception of the classification of ledger accounts it frequently occurs that the accounts are opened in the order of the entries first giving rise to their creation, and consequently follow one another indiscriminately, and in taking off the trial balance in the order of ledger folios the real, nominal, personal and impersonal accounts are presented in one heterogeneous and shuffled list.

Before a business and financial statement can be prepared from such a trial balance it is necessary to pick out and group the accounts into three principal classifications, viz :

First—Real Accounts representing assets and liabilities, (other than trade customers' and creditors' open accounts,) such as cash, properties, bills receivable, bills payable, mortgages payable, special personal accounts, etc.

Second—Nominal accounts representing profits and losses, such as purchases, sales, discounts, expenses, etc.

Third—Individual Accounts of trade debtors and creditors (this classification usually comprises by far the greatest number of accounts) constituting two schedules termed respectively "open book accounts receivable" and "open book accounts payable."

In a properly arranged ledger the accounts would follow in the order of the foregoing classification, by having separate sections of the ledger allotted to each ; but in the absence of such an arrangement the same purpose may be accomplished so far as the trial balance is concerned, by taking off the balances on three different sheets, or extending the amounts into three separate pairs of columns, thus effecting the requisite classification.

A trial balance so arranged not only facilitates the preparation of a Revenue Statement and Balance Sheet, but presents the accounts in such form that deductions may be drawn and approximate results shown without the compilation of formal statements at interim dates.

Q. 10.   Define and differentiate :

(a) Fixed Assets and Cash Assets.

(b) Fixed Liability and Floating Indeptedness.

(c) Fixed Charges and Operating Expenses.

A. 10. (a) Fixed assets are those which form the plant and permanent equipment of a business and must be maintained in their efficiency by repairs and renewals in order to successfully carry on its undertakings. The roadway, buildings and rolling stock of a railroad, the land, buildings, machinery and fittings of a manufacturing concern, are fixed assets, as well as patent rights, franchises, and in some instances good will, when the same are carried upon the books as asset values.

Cash Assets, also called floating assets, are those which are either subject to change arising from business transactions, or may be sold, exchanged, or otherwise realized upon, without detracting from the appliances or facilities necessary to the business uses and operations. Cash, stock in trade, customers' accounts, bills receivable, securities, or any assets held subject to sale or to realization in cash, are floating assets ; and to the extent that they are available or their collection is relied upon for funds to liquidate current obligations they constitute working capital.

(b) Fixed Liabilities are the permanent or ultimate obligations as distinct from the current obligations (or floating indebtedness) of a person, firm or corporation.   Mortgages upon realty or chattels, and the share or loan capital of a corporation are forms of fixed liability.

Floating Indebtedness consists of all liabilities that are due and payable at once or currently becoming so, as they severally mature.

Trade creditors' book accounts, bills payable, accrued rents, rates and taxes, interest payable, and salaries or wages owing to employees constitute items of floating indebtedness.

(c) Fixed Charges are expenses inevitably occurring at regular intervals and in determined amounts, and constitute a regularly established and approximately uniform charge to revenue, year by year. Interest on funded debt, state tax on capital stock, tax on franchise, or rents, rates and taxes on realty are subjects of fixed charges.

Operating Expenses are those incidental to the active operations of a business and vary in amount with their expansion or contraction. The term is applied most frequently to railroad, telegraph, telephone, steamship and transportation companies or common carriers generally, where their accounts do not admit of the distinction between trading and general management charges characteristic of manufacturing and mercantile industries.

Q. 11. Describe the following kinds of accounts :

(a) Personal,   (b) Impersonal,

(c) Real,   (d) Nominal,

(e) Current,   (f) Summary.

A. 11. (a) Personal Accounts, also termed "individual accounts," are accounts stating the transactions between a business and its various debtors and creditors, each account showing the claim or liability, with respect to such transactions, of the party whose name it bears. John Brown in % with Henry Smith, Henry Smith's Capital Account, Henry Smith's Drawing Account are types of personal accounts.

(b) Impersonal Accounts are accounts in no way involving or stating any personal credit or indebtedness, but are maintained for the purpose of recording the transactions of a business with respect to the properties acquired or parted with, the various sources of income, and the subjects of expenditure. Real Estate, Mortgages, Commissions, Purchases, Sales, Expenses, Profit and Loss are types of impersonal accounts.

(c) Real Accounts are those which state the value of actual assets or extent of actual liabilities and may be either personal or impersonal. Cash, Land, Buildings, Machinery, Mortgages, either receivable or payable, Bills Receivable, Bills Payable, and Individual Accounts receivable and payable are types of real accounts.

(d) Nominal Accounts are accounts in name only and represent neither personal interest or obligation, nor asset or liability values, but are maintained solely for the purpose of classifying profits and losses under various speculative or generic headings, growing out of established theory and usage, which accounts are closed at the end of each fiscal period by transferring the balances to Profit and Loss account, Revenue account or whatever account may constitute the summary or resume of the business.   Trading, Interest, Discount, Commissions, Rents Rates and Taxes, Insurance, Advertising, Wages, Salaries, and Expense are types of nominal accounts.

(e) A Current Account, or account current, (%) also termed a "running account," is an itemized account, wherein all the items of transactions are recorded in the order of their dates.   A personal account is generally an account current, as John Brown in % with Henry Smith.

(f) A Summary Account (acct.) is an account wherein each item is the aggregate of some other account or statement of particulars.   A Profit and Loss account is a type of a summary account.

Some accounts partake in a sense of the nature of both current and summary, as for instance, a Sales Account is credited monthly with the total sales from the sales book, each entry being a summary for its respective month but following each other in current order.

Q. 12.   Describe the process and state some of the pur· poses of analyzing a ledger.

A. 12.   The analysis of a ledger is accomplished by distributing the elements of each account in turn throughout a series of Dr. and Cr. columns upon a working paper called "an analysis sheet."

Beginning with the Dr. or Cr. balance, if any, of each account at the commencement of the period under analysis, it is entered in its re· spective column on the extreme left hand of the analysis sheet.

The amounts charged to each account for the period are entered item by item in a series of debit columns, each column being allotted to one of the several books of original entry from which the items are posted, to wit, sales book, journal, cash book, etc., and the page of the book of original entry is noted against each item.

The amounts credited to each account are correspondingly entered item by item, in a series of credit columns, each column being allotted to one of the several books of original entry from which the items are posted, to wit, invoice book, journal, cash book, etc., and the page of the book of original entry is noted against each item.

The Dr. or Cr. balance, if any, at the end of the period under analysis is finally entered in its respective column on the extreme right of the analysis sheet.

Each account will then extend across the analysis sheet and occupy as many lines as there are items in the column containing the greatest number of items.

The accounts follow one under the other in the order of the ledger folios, each commencing on the first clear line across the analysis sheet, and the debit balances together with the debit items will equal the credit balances together with the credit items, and the balancing of the work as it progresses will be always under control.

At the completion of each analysis sheet the columns are all footed and the sheet balanced and agreed.

When the analysis of the ledger is completed, the footings of all the analysis sheets are summarized for a grand total and the balances at the commencement and at the conclusion of the period will total and agree with the trial balance schedules taken off at the respective dates, while the intermediate columns connecting the commencing with the concluding balances will severally agree with the total footings of the books of original entry to which they respectively relate, and may be checked back therewith by means of the page notations for any disagreement that they may reveal.

The purposes of such analysis are :

First—A sure expedient for arriving at a perfect balance of a ledger wherein the accounts are so numerous, the figures so illegible, the errors of so treacherous a nature, and the chronological order of the items so imperfect as to baffle the usual method of checking postings and retaking off of the trial balance.

Second.—Acquiring possession of a transcript of all items in a ledger, during an investigation, where only temporary access to the books is granted by a court order, and the interests of a client render it advisable.

Q. 13. Describe the nature of the following accounts :

(a)   Sinking fund.

(b)   Reserve fund.

(c)   Redemption fund.

(d)   Depreciation fund.

(e)   Contingent fund.

(f)   Investment fund.

A. 13. (a) A Sinking Fund, in its strictly technical sense is formed by the setting apart and accumulating of moneys by a government to make provision for paying interest on its debts and ultimately discharging them. The payments into it are fixed in amount, are made at regular intervals and are invested and the interest therefrom added to the fund to the end that the amounts paid in, together with the accumulated income thereon will provide a certain required amount at a given date. The term is frequently used erroneously in commercial accounts in the place of reserve fund, redemption fund or depreciation fund ; but whereas the latter accounts invariably show credit balances set aside out of profits, a sinking fund shows a debit balance representing an aggregation of specific asset values.

(b)   A Reserve Fund is an amount set aside from time to time out of profits (by a charge to revenue and credit to reserve) with or without a distinct object in view, and in the latter case available for any ulterior purpose, such as equalization of dividends, meeting of exceptional losses, etc.; but if to provide for any definite and anticipated contingency it is generally more specifically styled, as, for example, "reserve for bad debts, reserve for discounts," etc., and is in such cases usually alluded to as a "reserve account." Whereas in the cases of sinking and contingent funds, specific and available asset values are represented, a reserve fund simply represents in part the surplus of aggregate assets over aggregate liabilities.

(c) A Redemption Fund is an amount set aside out of profits in yearly or other periodical installments (by a charge to revenue and a credit to redemption fund) which by the time a certain funded debt or other obligation matures will equal the principal sum thereof and provide an accumulated surplus for its redemption. It is practically the payment of a time loan out of revenue, by charging a proportion of said loan against the profits of each year over which it extends, and expresses the amount of surplus as and when set aside for such purpose in a separate account as "Bond Redemption Account," "First Mortgage Redemption Account," etc. This account is similar in character to a reserve fund, inasmuch as it represents undivided profits without regard to any specific asset values and appears as a credit account in the ledger. In all such accounts the sinking fund principle is understood to comprehend all available assets (whether constituting special investments or otherwise), which contribute to the general surplus of which this account represents the amount set aside and accumulated for redemption of the debt provided for.

(d) A Depreciation Fund is an amount set aside out of profits (by a charge to revenue and credit to depreciation) requisite to offset the decreased value of plant, machinery, and other properties, occasioned by wear-and-tear and other causes. Against this fund is charged the cost of such properties as become extinct as well as partial decrease in value as determined or estimated. Depreciation is frequently provided for by a direct credit to the property accounts as against the charge to revenue, which process is technically termed "writing down assets" as the antithesis to the expression "writing up assets," which latter implies increasing their book value without actual addition thereto ; as in the case of rising value in land due to local development being taken avail of upon the books as an offset to extraordinary shrinkages and losses in ther directions.

(e) A Contingent Fund is formed by setting aside either a stated ortion of the general receipts, or such receipts as are not specable to or held for other purposes. The object of such fund or the payment of incidental expenses not anticipated in ided for by other funds similarly set aside. It is used cal government institutions as well as to charitable and social organizations, and inasmuch as it is an actual accumulation of funds and appears as an asset or debtor account upon the books it resembles a sinking fund. The term "contingent fund," when used (as it often is) in place of "reserve fund," is a technical error, occasioned by a careless and indiscriminate use of terms and the absence of a due sense of that accuracy of expression and careful discrimination in the nomenclature of accountancy which should characterise the work of a professional accountant.

(f)   An Investment Fund is an amount set aside out of profits (by a charge to revenue and credit to investment) for the purchase of securities that can be quickly realized upon in times of monetary stringency, when the ordinary resources of the business may become tied up in slow assets and the liabilities at the same time be quick and urgent.   There are two methods of treating with this fund upon the books ; one method is for the investment fund to appear among the liabilities as a reserve account, and the corresponding securities purchased therewith to appear among the assets ; the other method is to charge the securities purchased out of said fund to the fund itself, and show upon the balance sheet among the liabilities only the balance of the fund remaining uninvested, in which case the fund forms the subject of a separate statement accompanying the balance sheet and revenue account.

Q. 14.   Define the following :

(a) Stock.

(b) Capital.

(c) Surplus.

(d) Deficiency.

(e) Capital Stock.

(f) Preferred Stock.

(g) Common Stock.

(h) Share Capital.

(i) Loan Capital.

A. 14. (a)   The term "Stock" without further qualificatio frequently used as the heading of the capital account of a single p etor or partners in a firm ; also the goods or merchandise dealt business, the expression "taking stock" having reference to the act of inspecting and making inventory of the wares unsold at the end of a fiscal period. The capital stock of a corporation is frequently spoken of simply as "stock," and the brokers dealing therein are known as stock brokers.

(b) The term "Capital" without further qualification signifies the principal invested or remaining in a business, and is a more acceptable title to the account of a proprietor's interest in a business than "stock," which in this application is becoming obsolete. The capital stock of a corporation is frequently spoken of in the aggregate simply as "capital," and the amount to which it is limited by the certificate of incorporation is known as the "authorized capital," as distinct from "paid in capital" the amount actually issued.

(c) The term "Surplus" without further qualification signifies the remaining assets or funds of any business or estate after all claims, liabilities and obligations have been provided for. It is sometimes specifically qualified, as surplus assets, surplus cash, surplus income, in which cases its significance is accordingly limited.

(d) The term "Deficiency" without further qualification signifies the insufficiency of the assets or funds of a business or estate to meet, discharge or satisfy its claims, liabilities or obligations.

(e) The term "Capital Stock" signifies the amount for which a company or corporation is authorized to issue its share certificates for value received from subscribers thereto ; the aggregate par value of the certificates issued ; the liability to stockholders by virtue of said certificates ; the certificates themselves.

(f) Preferred Stock is a form of capital stock, vesting in the holders thereof prior rights to the assets in the event of liquidation and insuring to them a stated dividend in preference to the holders of common stock, and frequently including other provisions which are the subjects of special contracts.

(g) Common Stock is the general form of capital stock, vesting in the holders thereof the usual proprietary rights in the assets, earnings and voting privileges commonly implied, without any special form of contract beyond the bare acknowledgement of the amount subscribed.

(h)   Share Capital is a general term applied to both preferred and common stock, conveying the idea of proprietary interest in the business with its attendant liability, as distinct from loan capital.

(i)   Loan Capital is a general term applied to capital borrowed by a company or corporation upon its bonds secured by mortgage upon its properties, but conveying to the obligees no proprietary rights or voting privileges in the management of its affairs.

Q. 15. Describe the nature of the following accounts :

(a)   Merchandise.

(b)   Construction.

(c)   Consignment.

(d)   Joint.

(e)   Subscription.

(f)   Expense.

(g)   Maintenance.

(h)   Venture.

(i)   Suspense.

(j)   Dividend.

A. 15. (a)   Merchandise is the title of an account almost universally met with in the books of concerns engaged in the buying and selling of commodities and deals with the subjects of purchases, sales, returns, allowances and other offsets, also with freights, duties, and sometimes labor of manufacturing; and being charged and credited with the inventories at its opening and close respectively, embraces in one running account the transactions mainly contributing to a trading account.   As it is necessary to analyze a merchandise account into its different elements just enumerated before a clear and summarized statement of the transactions it includes may be adequately expressed, the merchandise account as first described is open to well-grounded objections ; therefore in advanced systems of accounting it is giving place to a group of separate accounts each dealing with but one of its principal elements, and which when ultimately assembled constitute a general trading account in summarized form.

(b) Construction is either the title of an account or a general term applied to a series of accounts dealing with cost of building and equipping railroads, canals, ships, buildings or other public or private works, and recording the value thereof when completed.

(c) A Consignment Account is an account opened by a merchant who is the consignee, for recording the sales, charges and commissions incidental to the disposition of goods belonging to and received from another merchant who is the consignor, and for whose account and risk the goods are received and sold. The corresponding account on the books of the consignor is called a "shipment account", but is sometimes alluded to as "consigment outward" in which case the consignment account proper on the books of the consignee is distinguished by the term "consignment inward". The statement which the consignee renders to the consignor upon remitting the proceeds or transferring the same to the consignor's account current is called an "account sales".

(d) A Joint Account records the transactions of some particular enterprise of a temporary nature where several parties combine in contributing requisite capital and services, and share in the profits or losses. Where the enterprise is of a commercial nature involving shipments and consignments (on joint account) between the parties concerned, it is termed a "joint venture" or "joint adventure".

(e) Subscription Account is a general term for all accounts recording the written pledges of a number of parties underwriting to a scheme, in which they agree to contribute or at the time do contribute money or other value in consideration for something received or to be received. It is used in corporations with respect to the capital stock, in publishing houses with respect to the sale of special literary productions, and appears in many forms of business in respect of various enterprises.

(f) Expense is either the title of an account or a general term applied to a series of accounts for recording the expenditures incidental to the management of a business or enterprise, for which no permanent, subsequently convertible, or substantial value is received, as for instance, rent, insurance, clerk hire, etc.

(g) Maintenance is either the title of an account, or the term applied to a series of accounts for recording the cost of repairing, renewing, replacing, and in a general way keeping up the efficiency and service-ability of fixed assets.

(h) Venture Account, or, as it is sometimes termed, "adventure account", is a title frequently applied to specific shipments on consignment when made the subject of separate accounts. If at the risk and on behalf of the shipper as co-partner with others, the account is called a "joint venture" and is a form of joint account.

(i) Suspense is the title of an account opened for the purpose of posting thereto such items concerning which the exact nature or ultimate treatment is not known at the time the entries are made, by reason of dispute pending settlement, claims in litigation, or other causes which may render it inexpedient to definitely construe the premises, or commit such construction until further developments or adjudication by the courts. The same title is frequently given to bad debts account, to which is carried the balances of customers' accounts concerning which hope of collection is in suspense or has been abandoned, and which it is advisable to remove from the active accounts in the ledger.

(j) Dividend is the title of an account on the books of a corporation to which is credited each dividend as declared, and against which is charged the payments thereof as made. Where the stockholders are numerous it is customary to open an account for each dividend, so that the amount owing upon each dividend remaining unpaid after subsequent dividends have been declared, will appear separately stated and each dividend will be separately liquidated.

PRACTICAL ACCOUNTING.

PRACTICAL ACCOUNTING.

Q. 1. Jones & Robinson, merchants, are unable to meet their obligations. From their books and the testimony of the insolvent debtors the following statement of their condition is ascertained :

Cash on hand, ...	$ 5,500 00
Debtors: $1,000 good; $600 doubtful, but estimated to produce $200;	
$1,000 bad, ...	2,600 00
Property, estimated to produce $9,000, ...	14,000 00
Bills receivable, good, ...	4,250 00
Other securities: $3,000 pledged with partially secured creditors; remainder held by fully secured creditors, ...	28,000 00
Jones, drawings, ...	9,000 00
Robinson, drawings, ...	8,400 00
Sundry losses, ...	13,500 00
Trade expenses, ...	7,400 00
Creditors, unsecured	25,000 00
Creditors, partially secured	23,900 00
Creditors, fully secured, ...	17,000 00
Preferential claims; wages, salaries and taxes, ...	700 00
Jones, capital, ...	10,000 00
Robinson, capital, ...	16,050 00

Prepare a statement of affairs, showing the liabilities and the assets with respect to their realization and liquidation ; also a deficiency account showing such of the above stated particulars as would account for the deficiency shown by the statement of affairs.

A. 1.　　STATEMENT OF AFFAIRS, 15TH DECEMBER, 1896, JONES & ROBINSON.

Total Liabilities.	LIABILITIES.		Expected to Rank.
$25,000 00	Creditors, unsecured, per schedule A		$25,000 00
23,900 00	Creditors, partly secured, per schedule B	$23,900 00	
	Securities at estimated value.	3,000 00	20,900 00
17,000 00	Creditors, fully secured, per schedule C	17,000 00	
	Securities at estimated value	25,000 00	
	Surplus to contra,	8,000 00	
	Preferential creditors, for wages, salaries, taxes, etc., per schedule D		
700 00	Deducted contra,	700 00	
66,600 00			45,900 00

Nominal Assets.	ASSETS.		Estimated to Produce.
$5,500 00	Cash on hand,		$5,500 00
14,000 00	Property, per schedule E	$14,000 00	9,000 00
2,600 00	Sundry Debtors, per schedule F viz : Good,		1,000 00
	Doubtful,	600 00	200 00
	Bad,	1,000 00	
4,250 00	Bills receivable, per schedule G		4,250 00
28,000 00	Other securities in hands of creditors, partly secured,	3,000 00	
	fully secured,	25,000 00	
	Deducted contra,	28,000 00	
	Surplus from securities in the hands of creditors, fully secured, per contra,		8,000 00
			27,950 00
	Deduct preferential creditors, for wages, salaries, taxes etc., per contra,		700 00
			27,250 00
	Deficiency, as per Deficiency Acct.,		18,650 00
54,350 00			45,900 00

A. 1.—Continued. DEFICIENCY ACCOUNT—JONES & ROBINSON.

To Deficiency as shown by Statement of Affairs,		$18,650 00	By Losses on Trading, viz:		
			Sundry Losses,	$13,500 00	
" Capital brought into the business at commencement, and since, viz:			Trade Expenses,	7,400 00	$20,900 00
Jones, capital,	$10,000 00		" Losses and Shrinkage in Values, as exhibited by Statement of Affairs, viz: Property,		
Robinson, capital,	16,050 00	26,050 00		5,000 00	
			Debtors, Doubtful,	400 00	
			do Bad,	1,000 00	6,400 00
			" Drawings from the business, viz:		
			Jones, drawings,	9,000 00	
			Robinson, "	8,400 00	17,400 00
		44,700 00			44,700 00

Q. 2. A, B and C enter into partnership January 1, 1895. A contributes $8,500, B $5,500, and C $4,500. The profits and losses are to be divided in the same proportion. December 31, 1895, the partners agree that before dividing profits and losses there shall be charged as an expense of the business and placed to their individual credit, salaries as follows : A $800, B $700, C $600.

December 31, 1895, the trial balance of their books showed the following :

Capital, A,		$8,500 0
Capital, B,		5,500 00
Capital, C,		4,500 00
Cash on hand and in bank,	$1,900 48	
Stock, January 1, 1895,	11,550 00	
Purchases,	51,666 70	
Sales,		25,650 80
Plant and fixtures,	2,068 92	
Book accounts receivable, including consignments,	20,745 83	
Consignments,		33,822 70
Trade Creditors,		14,855 66
Loan account,		6,250 00
Loan interest,		125 00
Salaries,	1,257 00	
Wages,	2,025 00	
Trading expenses,	1,052 65	
Interest and discount,	1,273 45	
Losses on exchange,	2,108 00	
Commissions,		3,510 20
Drawings, A, (includes $300, salary allowance)	2,750 25	
Drawings, B, (includes $700, salary allowance)	2,345 65	
Drawings C, (includes $600, salary allowance)	1,970 43	
	$102,714 36	$102,714 36

Their inventory of stock on hand December 31, 1895, amounted to $11,337.50. Unexpired insurance premiums $91. December 31, 1895, $300 was paid for January (1896) rent in advance.

Prepare a trading account (cost as against proceeds), a profit and loss account and a balance sheet, also partners' capital accounts as of December 31, 1895, allowing 6 per cent. interest on capital and reserving 2½ per cent. for losses on consignments.

A. 2.

TRADING ACCOUNT OF THE BUSINESS OF A, B & C,
For the year ending 31st December, 1895.

Ledger fol.		Cost.			Proceeds.	
	To Stock on hand 1st Jan., '95,	$11,550 00		By sales,		$25,650 80
	" Purchases,	51,666 70		" on consignment,	33,822 70	33,061 69
	" Wages,	2,025 00		Deduct reserve 2½ %	761 01	
		65,241 70				
	Deduct Inventory, 31st Dec., '95.	11,337 50				
		53,904 20				
	Balance, being Gross Profit, carried to Profit and Loss Acct.,	4,808 29				58,712 49
		58,712 49				58,712 49

PROFIT AND LOSS ACCOUNT OF THE BUSINESS OF A, B & C,
For the year ending 31st December, 1895.

Ledger fol.						
	To Trade Expenses,		$1,052 65	By Gross Profits from trading account		$4,808 29
	Deduct Unexpred Ins.,	91.00		" Commissions,		3,510 20
	Jan., '96, Rent, paid in advance,	300 00	391 00			
			661 65			
	" Losses on Exchange,		2,108 00			
	" Interest and Discount,		1,273 45			
	" Salaries of Clerks,		1,257 00			8,318 49
			5,300 10			
	" Balance carried down,		3,018 39			
			8,318 49			
	To Interest on Capital, 1 yr.,			By Balance brought down,		3,018 39
	A, $8,500 @ 6 %	510 00		" Net loss, after charging interest on capital and partners' salaries, divisible as under,		
	B, 5,500 @ "	330 00				
	C, 4,500 @ "	270 00	1,110 00			
	" Partners' Salaries, 1 yr.,			A, 17/37,	88 04	
	A, salary,	800 00		B, 11/37,	56 96	
	B, "	700 00		C, 9/37,	46 61	191 61
	C, "	600 00	2,100 00			
			3,210 00			3,210 00

A. 2.—*Continued.*

BALANCE SHEET, 31st DECEMBER, 1895, OF A. B & C.

Ledger fol.	Assets.			Ledger fol.	Liabilities.		
	Cash,	$2,068 92	$1,900 48		Trade Creditors,	$6,250 00	$14,355 66
	Properties, as under Plant and Fixtures,	11,337 50	13,406 42		Loan Account,	125 00	6,375 00
	Inventory of Stock,	91 00			Interest,		
	Prepaid charges, as under Insurance Premiums,	300 00					
	Rent for January, 1896,		391 00				21,230 66
	Book accts. Receivable,	20,745 83			Capital, A,	6,971 71	
	Deduct Reserve 2½% on 33,822.70,	761 01	19,984 82		B,	4,127 39	
			35,082 72		C,	3,352 96	14,152 06
			35,082 72				35,682 72

"A." CAPITAL ACCOUNT.

1895					1895				
Dec.	31	To Drawings,	$2,750 25		Jan.	1	By Capital, investment,	$8,500 00	
"	"	" Profit and Loss, 17.3% of $191.61,	88 04		Dec.	31	" Interest on do. 1 year @ 6%	510 00	
"	"	" Balance, carried down,	6,971 71		"	"	" Salary,	800 00	
			9,810 00					9,810 00	
					1896 Jan.	1	By balance, brought down.	6,971 71	

"B." CAPITAL ACCOUNT.

1895					1895				
Dec.	31	To Drawings,	$2,345 65		Jan.	1	By Capital, investment,	$5,500 00	
"	"	" Profit and Loss 11.3% of $191.61,	56 96		Dec.	31	" Interest on do. 1 year @ 6%	330 00	
"	"	" Balance, carried down,	4,127 39		"	"	" Salary,	700 00	
			6,530 00					6,530 00	
					1896 Jan.	1	By Balance, brought down.	4,127 39	

"C." CAPITAL ACCOUNT.

1895					1895				
Dec.	31	To Drawings,	$1,970 43		Jan.	1	By Capital, investment,	$4,500 00	
"	"	" Profit and Loss, 9.3% of $191.61,	46 61		Dec.	31	" Interest on do. 1 year @ 6%	270 00	
"	"	" Balance, carried down,	3,352 96		"	"	" Salary,	600 00	
			5,370 00					5,370 00	
					1896 Jan.	1	By Balance, brought down.	3,352 96	

Q. 3. A buys a gas business at receiver's sale, taking over the entire plant, subject to a bonded indebtedness of $9,500. A sells the same to the B Gas Company, incorporated under the laws of the State of New York for the purpose of acquiring this property from him, and having an authorized capital of $30,000, divided into 300 shares of $100 each. C, D and E subscribe each for one share of the capital stock of the company, and the company purchases the property from A for 297 shares and assumes the bonded indebtedness stated.

On making and appraising an inventory of the property for the purpose of distribution to proper accounts, the following conservative values, exclusive of good will, franchise, rights, etc., are ascertained:

Land, ...	$2,000 00
Buldings, ...	6,000 00
Coal-gas plant, machinery and fittings, ...	3,800 00
Water-gas plant, machinery and fittings, ...	6,000 00
Mains, ...	27,000 00
Meters, ...	1,200 00
Supplies, ...	1,500 00
Office furniture and fixtures, ...	300 00
Sundry other items, ...	1,200 00
	$49,000 00

Frame the necessary entries to open the company's books and show the capital stock and fixed assets on the face of the ledger. Prepare a balance sheet.

A. 3.   CASH BOOK ENTRIES.

To Capital Stock, "C."	Certif. No.	1.	$100	00	
" " "D."	" "	2.	100	00	
" " "E."	" "	3.	100	00	

A. 8.—Continued.   JOURNAL ENTRIES.

The "B" Gas Company of........ .... incorporated under the laws of the State of New York, ...189 Authorized Capital, $30,000. 300 Shares, par value $100 each.			
Plant and Sundry Assets, Comprising Land, Buildings, Gas Machinery, Mains, Fittings, Meters, Supplies, Consumers' Accounts, and other properties comprehended in connection with the franchise and Gas Business, situated at................ ......N. Y.	$39,200 00		
TO SUNDRIES, AS UNDER. *"A" Vendor.* For transfer to this Company by the above vendor, of his entire equity in the above described assets as of...... ....189 by Bill of sale bearing date ...., duly executed and acknowledged, and pursuant to resolution of the Board of Directors held this day, and entered in Minutes, page......		$ 9,700 00	
Bond and Mortgage %s. .... bonds of $......each, upon the above stated plant and sundry assets, bearing interest @ .... % payable semi-annually on ...... and ......, and assumed by this Company as part consideration, pursuant to a resolution of the Board of Directors at a meeting held this day and appearing upon page...... of the minutes.		9,500 00	
"A" Vendor. To *Capital Stock.* Certificates Nos. .... for 297 shares of the full paid Capital Stock of this Company, issued to the above named vendor, in consideration of, and as the purchase price for his equity in the plant and sundry assets stated in the foregoing entry, pursuant to a resolution, recited therein.	$29,700 00	$29,700 00	
SUNDRIES, To Plant and Sundry Assets, Land, as per schedule, Buildings, " Coal-Gas Plant, Machinery and Fittings, " Water-Gas Plant, Machinery and Fittings, " Mains, " Meters, " Supplies, " Office Furniture and Fixtures, " Sundry other items (per stated accounts), "	2,000 00 6,000 00 3,800 00 6,000 00 27,000 00 1,200 00 1,500 00 300 00 1,200 00	49,000 00	
For distribution to specific accounts to be hereafter maintained, of the property taken over by this Company at the aggregate valuation of $39,200.00, subject to a Mortgage of $9,500. for which there was issued 297 shares of the stock of this Company, in consideration for the equity thus acquired. Details of valuations and appraisals by Mr. .... are more fully set forth in Schedules of Particulars, duly entered in the Inventory and Depreciation Register.			

NOTE.—The increase arising, by the above appraisal value, over and above the aggregate sum of $39,200, (which is exclusive of Franchise Rights, Good Will, or any speculative value whatsoever), and which increase now stands at the Credit of Plant and Sundry Assets Acct.; although constituting a clear surplus, is not however properly available for dividends, and should stand as a reserve.

A. 3—*Continued.*   LEDGER ENTRIES (Postings).

DR.				Capital Stock.			CR.
				By Cash C, Certif., No. 1,	"		$100 00
				" " D, " 2,	"		100 00
				" " E, " 3,	"		100 00
				" A Vendor "	J		29,700 00

Bond and Mortgage—% Int. due.................&.................

				By Plant and Sundry Assets.	J		9,500 00

"A" Vendor.

To Capital Stock,			$29,700 00	By Plant and Sundry Assets.	J		29,700 00

Plant and Sundry Assets.

To Sundries,	J	39,200 00		By Sundries,	J		49,000 00

Land.

To Plant and Sundry Assets.	J	2,000 00					

Buildings.

To Plant and Sundry Assets,	J	6,000 00					

Coal-Gas Plant, Machinery and Fittings.

To Plant and Sundry Assets.	J	3,800 00					

Water-Gas Plant, Machinery and Fittings.

To Plant and Sundry Assets,	J	6,000 00					

Mains.

To Plant and Sundry Assets,	J	27,000 00					

Meters.

To Plant and Sundry Assets,	J	1,200 00					

Supplies.

To Plant and Sundry Assets.	J	1,500 00					

Office Furniture and Fixtures.

To Plant and Sundry Assets.	J	300 00					

Sundry Other Items (Accounts not stated).

To Plant and Sundry Assets.	J	1,200 00					

BALANCE SHEET OF THE "B" GAS COMPANY.

A. 3.—Continued.

ASSETS.			LIABILITIES.		
Cash,	$ 300	00	Capital Stock, 300 shares at $100,	$30,000	00
Land,	2,000	00	Bond and Mortgage,	9,500	00
Buildings,	6,000	00	Plant and Sundry Assets, being a		
Coal-Gas Plant, Mchy. and Fittings,	3,800	00	Surplus arising from excess of		
Water-Gas Plant, Mchy. and Fittings,	6,000	00	appraised value over cost, and		
Mains,	27,000	00	held as a special reserve,	9,800	00
Meters,	1,200	00			
Supplies,	1,500	00			
Office Furniture and Fixtures,	300	00			
Sundry other items,	1,200	00			
	49,300	00		49,300	00

Q. 4. Three partners invest capital as follows: A, $100,000; B, $60,000; C, $40,000. On this basis of capital investment *which is to remain intact*, they share profits and losses in the proportion of A, 47½ %, B, 27½ %, C, 25 %, in addition to specified salaries.

At the end of the year the partnership terminates with a loss of $10,000, which includes the salaries drawn by the partners. It appears that C had drawn against prospective profits to the amount of $5,000, and thereby impaired his capital investment by said amount. They discontinue business and proceed to liquidate and distribute the surplus assets monthly as realized. C engages in other business, leaving A and B to attend to the realization and liquidation of the firm's affairs. A and B jointly are to charge C 5 % for collecting and paying to him his share in the surplus assets.

The amounts collected monthly, less liabilities liquidated and expenses and losses on realization (exclusive of the 5 % collection charged to C, the amount of which is to be equally divided between A and B) are as follows:

First month, ...	$20,250.50
Second month, ...	30,490,75
Third month, ...	60,890.25
Fourth month, ...	58,725.10
Fifth month, ...	6,717.68
Last month, ...	4,425.72
	$181,500.00

Prepare partners' accounts showing the amounts payable monthly to each without prejudice to the rights or individual interests of the others.

A. 4.

"A" ACCOUNT.

To Share of Losses, 47½% of $10,000,		$4,750	00	By Capital Investment, 50 %,		$100,000	00
" Cash, 1st Month, 12½% of Capital.		12,500	00				
" " " " on a/c		250	50				
" " 2d " to bring Capital to 47½%		20,749	50				
" Balance, carried down,		61,750	00				
		100,000	00			100,000	00
" Cash, 3d Month,	47½%	26,899	96	By Balance brought down	= 47½%	61,750	00
" " " " 2½% Collection Ch'ge a/c C		353	94	" 3d Month, 2½% Collection Ch'ge a/c C	$14,157.87	353	94
" " 4th "	"	27,894	42	" 4th " " " " " "	14,681.28	367	03
" " " " " " " "		367	03	" 5th " " " " " "	1,679.42	41	99
" " 5th "	"	3,190	90	" Last " " " " " "	1,106.43	27	66
" " " " " " " "		41	99				
" " Last "	"	2,102	22				
" " " " " " " "	"	27	66				
" Liquidation Loss and Expense, $3,500,	"	1,662	50				
		62,540	62			62,540	62

"B" ACCOUNT.

To Share of Losses 27½ % of $10,000,		$ 2,750	00	By Capital Investment, 30 %		$60,000	00
" Cash, 1st Month, 12½ % of Capital,		7,500	00				
" " 2d. " to bring Capital to 27½ %		9,741	25				
" " 3rd " " " " " "		4,258	75				
" Balance, carried down		35,750	00				
		60,000	00			60,000	00
To Cash, 3rd month,	27½ %	15,573	67	By Balance brought down,	27½ %	35,750	00
" " " " 2½ % Collection Ch'ge a/c C		353	95	" 3d month, 2½ % Collection Ch'gs a/c C,	$14,157.87	353	95
" " 4th "	"	16,149	40	" 4th " " " " "	14,681.28	367	03
" " " " " " " " "		367	03	" 5th " " " " "	1,679.42	41	99
" " 5th "	"	1,847	36	" Last " " " " "	1,106.43	27	65
" " " " " " " " "		41	99				
" " Last "	"	1,217	07				
" " " " " " " " "		27	66				
" Liquidation Loss and Expense, $3500	"	962	50				
		36,540	63			36,540	63

A. 4.—Continued.

"C" ACCOUNT.

To Capital, withdrawn, (impairment 12½ %),			$5,000 00	By Capital Investment. 20 %.	$40,000 00
" Share of Losses, 25 %, $10,000,			2,500 00		
" Balance, carried down,			32,500 00		40,000 00
			40,000 00		
To Cash, 3d Month,	$13,449.98			By Balance brought down, 25 %	32,500 00
5 % Collection Ch'gs a/c A and B,	707.89 25 %	14,157 87			$32,500 00
	$13,947.22				
" " 4th "	734.06	14,681 28			
" " 5th "	1,595.44 / 88.98	1,679 42			
" " Last "	1,051.11 / 55.32	1,106 43			
" Liquidation, Loss and Expense $3,500		875 00			
		$32,500 00			

Q. 5.   On January 15, 1896, A of New York sent to B of London, account sales showing net proceeds due February 15, 1896, $17,500, and remitted 60 day sight exchange at $4.82 for balance of account.

A had, on November 15, 1895, invested $5,000 in a demand draft, exchange at $4.85, which he remitted to B, and on December 15, 1895, he had further remitted to B a 30 day date draft for £1759, 16s. 8d., exchange at $4.83, drawn on C. of London, who owed A $9000 on open account.   Interest to be calculated at 6% (360 day basis), London date 12 days subsequent to New York date.

Prepare account current as rendered by A. to B; also the accounts of B and C as they appear in A's ledger.

A. 5.   *"B" of London, in account current with "A" of New York.*   (*Form 1.*)

1896.   CR.

Jan. 15. By Net Proceeds, as per account sales rendered, due Feb. 15, 1896	$17,500.00	
Deduct 31 days interest @ 6 % Jan. 15, to Feb. 15, 1896,	90.42	
Cash Jan. 15, 1896		$17,409.58

1895.   DR.

Nov. 15, To Remittance, Demand Draft,	£1030 18/7 @ $4.85	$5,000.00
Interest Nov. 15, '95 to Jan. 15, 96, 61 days @ 6%		50.83
Dec. 15, " " 30 days date, Draft on C, London,	1759 16/8 @ 4.83	8,500.00
1896. Interest Dec. 15, '95 to Jan. 15, '96, 31 days @ 6%		43.92
Jan. 15. " " 60 days sight, Draft to balance	791 9/2 @ 4.82	3,814.83
	£3582 4/5	$17,409.58

E. & O. E.

New York, 15th January, 1896.

(Signed) A

Note Remittance, Nov. 15, '95, due in London, Nov, 27, '95

"   Dec. 15, '95 "   "   "   Jan. 14-17, '96

"   Jan. 15, '96 "   "   "   Mar. 28-31, '96

Above calculations of interest are according to custom, but exceed legal rate under laws of the State of New York, which is ½ % per calendar month.

A. 5—Continued.

"B." OF LONDON, IN ACCOUNT CURRENT WITH "A," OF NEW YORK. (Form II.)

DR.

1895		Amount.	Date of Value.	Days.	Int.
Nov. 15	To Remittance Demand Dft., £1,080, 18/7 @ $4.85	$5,000.00	Nov. 15	61	$50.83
Dec. 15	" Remittance 30 days date Draft, £1,759, 16/8 @ $4.83	8,500.00	Dec. 15	31	43.92
1896			1896		
Jan. 15	" Interest, as per Balance,	185.17	Contra		90.42
"	" Remittance 60 days sight, £791, 9/2 @ $4.82	3,814.83	Jan. 15		
	£3,582, 4/5	17,500.00			185.17

CR.

1895		Amount	Date of Value.	Days.	Int.
Jan. 15	By Net Proceeds, per acct. sales rendered,	$17,500.00	Feb. 15	31	90.42
	" Balance of Interest,				185.17
		17,500.00			185.17

E. & O. E.

New York, 15th January, 1896.

Signed A.

Note. Remittance, Nov. 15, '95; due in London Nov. 27, '95.
Dec. 15, '95; " " " Jan. 14-17, '96.
Jan. 15, '96; " " " Mar. 23-31, '96.

(A'S LEDGER.)

CONSIGNMENT ex. s/s ———— FOR ACCOUNT "B," LONDON.

DR.

1895				
Nov. 15	To Sundry Charges, Petties and Discounts,	C	......	
Dec. 15	" Cash, Demand Draft, £1,080, 18/7 @ $4.85		$5,000.00	
	" C. London, 30 d-date Draft, 1,759, 16/8 @ 4.83	J	8,500.00	
1896				
Jan. 15	" Interest, per acct. rendered,	J	185.17	
	" Cash, 60 d-sight Draft to balance, 791, 9/2 @ 4.82	C	3,814.83	

CR.

1895			
Dec. 15	By Sundry Sales (Gross),	......	$17,500.00
	" Net Proceeds,	......	

(A'S LEDGER.)

"C" OF LONDON.

DR.

1895					
....	To Balance,	£	O	.....	$9,000.00

CR.

1895		
Dec. 15	By Consignment acct. B, London, Dft. 30 d-date @ 4.83, £1,759, 16/8	$3,500.00

Q. 6. A, B, and C agree to purchase and sell coffee for their joint account.

They purchase 3,000 bags of coffee for $58,500, and one month thereafter sell the same at 16 cents per lb., (say 130 lbs. to the bag). The warehouse charges, labor, cartage, weighing, brokerage, etc., amuont to $600.

A contributes cash, ...		$20,000.00
B contributes note at 4 months, ...	$19,000.00	
Discount at 6% on same, ...	?	?
C contributes cash, ...		$18,900.00
C contributes note at 3 months, ...	2,500.00	
Discount at 6% on same, ...	?	?
		$59,982.50

It was arranged that each should contribute equally to the requisite purchase money, in default of which, interest at 6% per annum for the month covering the transaction was to be calculated between them, to equalize their respective contributions.

Prepare an account of the venture, also separate accounts of A, B and C, showing the share of each in the final net proceeds.

A, 6,—*Continued*.   VENTURE, 3,000 BAGS COFFEE FOR ACCOUNT OF A., B AND C.

To Purchase 3,000 Bags Coffee	$58,500 00		By Proceeds 3,000 Bags Coffee. 390,000 lbs. @ 16c. lb.	$62,400 00
" Warehouse Charges, Labor, Cartage, Weighing, Brokerage, etc.	600 00		" Interest 1 month @ 6 % on $880 a/c B.	4 40
" Interest 1 month @ 6 % on $500 a/c A.	7 50			
" Interest 1 month @ 6 % on $1,862.50 a/c C.	9 31			
	59,111 81			62,404 40
" A one-third share of profit, . . $1,097.53				
" B one-third share of profit, . . $1,097 53				
" C one-third share of profit, . . $1,097.53	3,292 59			
	62,404 40			62,404 40

"A" ACCOUNT.   Venture, 3,000 Bags Coffee.

To Balance, carried down,	$21,100 03		By Cash a/c ½ Interest, $19,500,	$20,000 00
			" Interest, 1 month @ 6 %, on $500,	2 50
			" One-third Share of Profit,	1,097 53
	21,100 03			21,100 03
			By Balance, brought down,	21,100 03

A. 6.—Continued.   "B" ACCOUNT.   Venture, 3,000 Bags Coffee.

To Interest, 1 month @ 6 % on 80,		$4	40		By Note, @ 4 mos., $19,000, Deduct 6%, 4 mos., 380,	$18,620	00
" Balance, carried down.		19,713	13		" One-Third Share of Profit,	1,097	53
		19,717	53			19,717	53
					By Balance, brought down,	19,713	13

" C " ACCOUNT.   Venture, 3,000 Bags Coffee.

To Balance, carried down,		22,469	34		By Cash,	$18,900	00
					" Note @ 3 mos., $2,500.00, Due @ 6 % 3 mos., 87.50,	2,462	50
					" Interest, 1 mo. on 1,862.56	9	31
					" One-Third Share of Profit,	1,097	53
		22,469	34			22,469	34
					By Balance, brought down,	22,469	34

AUDITING.

AUDITING.

Q. 1. Give a brief outline of the duties of an auditor, and of his responsibilities.

A. 1. In the absence of any legal or specific definement, the duties as well as the responsibilities of an auditor must be regarded from purely ideal and moral standpoints, and are accordingly subject to a wide range of variations corresponding to the many purposes of audit and the circumstances which contribute to its making. However, to the extent that interests demand, occasions afford or stipulations are made, it is the auditor's duty to conscientiously employ every faculty and exercise every precaution in protecting the honest rights of his clients, to arrive at the true facts and results disclosed by his examination of the accounts he is employed to audit and to report thereon impartially respecting all essential particulars.

The principal duties which an auditor is called upon to perform may be summarized as follows:

To review the accounts of business institutions for the purpose of detecting error, mismanagement, or fraud, or of passing upon and determining their accuracy.

To insure a proper compliance with the terms of partnership agreements, corporate powers, regulations and resolutions, and guard against the illegal declarations of dividends, over-issue of capital stock, inflation of assets, or other violations of recognized business principles.

To inspect all vouchers, contracts and other collateral evidence bearing upon the accounts, as well as securities, notes, deeds and other evidences in support of the assets appearing upon the balance sheet.

To prepare the balance sheet and the revenue account at the close of each fiscal period, showing thereon suitable provision for contingent losses, reserves, sinking funds, etc.

To certify to the correctness of the balance sheet. An auditor is responsible for the accuracy of his figures and statements according to the impressions conveyed by his certificate or report, and when means of verification are not afforded him and he accepts another's figures, he should be punctilious in giving full prominence to such fact.

An auditor is professionally culpable if he fails to detect a radical error or fraud, (through "taking for granted" what was susceptible of proof, in his desire to curtail his work for a fixed fee, or yielding to importunities designedly or mayhap innocently made), unless it has been expressly stipulated that the portion of the work in which the error occurred was without the scope of his investigation.

Q. 2. Explain the principal points to which an auditor should direct his attention in conducting the audit of the accounts of an incorporated company.

A. 2. In conducting the audit of the accounts of an incorporated company, the auditor, whether engaged at the instance of the directors or general stockholders, is in reality entrusted with the interests of the latter, and should direct his investigation with the view of guarding their interests paramount to every other consideration, and while the officers and directors may seek to conceal from him or give plausible complexion to certain premises or points of policy respecting their administration, it is his duty to exercise the utmost tact and persistency in discovering their true inwardness and importance. As he is ultimately required to certify to the correctness of the profit and loss account and the balance sheet, and thereby is responsible for their accuracy, he should thoroughly satisfy himself on the following points :

That anything properly chargeable to revenue has not been capitalized.

That profit and loss account is charged with adequate depreciation on properties subject thereto, with due proportion of any balance for organization expenses, expiring patent rights, good-will, etc., with proper provision for bad debts, discounts and similar contingencies, and with accruing liabilities such as rent, taxes, wages, etc., as to the portion accrued at the date of closing the accounts.

That the stock-in-trade has been inventoried at cost, and the full details are written and signed by the parties who actually took stock.

That the values of fixed assets, good-will, patent rights, investments, and book debts are fairly stated, and that all liabilities are included on the balance sheet.

In general, as to the profit and loss account, that the profit, if any, has been fairly earned, and as to the balance sheet, that the assets are not over-estimated and the liabilities are all stated.

Finally, that proper minutes have been kept of the proceedings of the directors' and stockholders' meetings, containing proper resolutions for all transactions calling therefor, that the record of stock issue and transfer is in order, and that all acts of the company have been "intra vires".

Q. 3. If the actual cash on hánd at the date of the balance sheet had not been verified by the auditor on the day of balancing, what method should be employed to prove its correctness before signing the accounts?

A. 3. The auditor should verify the actual cash on hand at the date he enters upon the audit, by agreeing the cash book balance with the cash in the possession of the cashier and the balance in bank as shown by the cheque books, the latter to be reconciled with the bank pass book as soon as written up. Then tracing backwards, all interim receipts and payments between the date of balancing the cash and the former date of closing the accounts should be checked and verified, keeping under separate control the transactions in the several bank accounts and the receipts and payments of currency or petty cash, which, if found correct in detail, will result in an accurate determining of the cash balance at the date of the balance sheet, in hand and in bank, the latter further confirmed by the cheque book balances of even date therewith.

Taking, for instance, any one of the bank accounts and after ascertaining that all deposits and cheques have been entered in the cash book at the date of entering upon the audit and the balance remaining in the bank proven by the pass book and uncleared vouchers, if from that balance there be deducted all deposits entered in the cash book subsequent to the date of the balance sheet, and added thereto all cheques drawn and entered in the cash book subsequent to the date of the balance sheet, the resultant amount will be the balance in said bank at the date of the balance sheet, and form one of the component parts of the general cash balance stated thereon.

Q. 4.   In an audit where an exhaustive detailed examination of the books is not stipulated, or not practicable, what examination is essential to insure their general correctness?

A. 4.   An audit under limitations may imply any degree of thoroughness from an exhaustive examination of every detail to a mere cursory review of generalities, the object of each particular audit and the opportunities afforded in each case governing the extent to which it may be carried.

However, to insure the general correctness of the accounts, the footings of all the books of original entry should be verified, journal entries of an exceptional character scrutinized, and the postings to all nominal, representative and special accounts, both as to aggregate amounts and separate items, should be checked. An audit, to be at all effective, should also include the examination of vouchers for all cash payments and the verification of the final cash balance.

While such an audit is distinguished by the omission to check the postings to the individual customers' and creditors' accounts throughout, it is practicable where advanced systems of bookkeeping are employed to agree them in the aggregate, and it is advisable in any event to call over a few of the postings to the individual accounts covering a day here and there, and in like manner to examine invoices for purchases, and check extensions for a partial test of their accuracy.

Q. 5.   What means should be employed to detect the wilful omission to enter in the books under audit, sales made or cash received?

A. 5.   Considering the question from an extreme standpoint and assuming the utter absence of any record, direct or indirect, of sales made or cash received, and that the same relate to transactions with customers having accounts upon the books, the most effective way to detect default in making the entries is for the auditor, personally, to send to all customers statements of account, asking to be notified at his own address in case of any error or irregularity. By reason of the expense incurred by this expedient, it is seldom resorted to except when suspicion has been aroused that such wilful omission was being practiced, although the effectiveness and value of this measure should recommend it to more general employment.

In the case of cash sales being unaccounted for and necessarily involving the simultaneous omission of the cash receipts therefor, the detection of any specific incident would rest entirely upon accidental discovery or the effectiveness of the internal check employed, and would not fall within the range of the auditor's observation. The general effect, however, of systematic and extended peculations would become manifest in the trading account where the gross profits bore a uniform percentage to the prime cost and their failure to reach such percentage would indicate either a failure to record proceeds or the stealing of goods out of stock, to which latter the appropriation of cash sales is equivalent.

In concerns where settlements with customers are of a complicated nature, involving sales, returns, payments on account, discount adjustments, and the settlement slips being receipted and returned, a review of the particulars would involve figuring and reference to correspondence to an extent that would preclude the probability of subsequent inquiry; by fraudulently entering the cash for less than the actual receipts and increasing the discount accordingly, not only will the customer's account. liquidate but the proceeds of cash sales may be appropriated and still duly appear entered in the cash book without disturbing the cash balance called for.

Again, where receipts from customers are appropriated and their accounts subsequently credited upon receipts from other customers whose accounts are in turn held open after payment, until the extent of the embezzlement causes numerous accounts to remain open after actual settlement, it is frequently necessary to procure copies of the deposit slips from the banks wherein the moneys have been lodged, in order to trace the correct amounts of the cheques received from customers, and prove the falsity of the cash book entries and particulars of the deposits in the cheque book where the same have been itemized to give apparent support to the amounts falsely substituted.

Q. 6. State what should be required of a company or firm by one who is to make an audit of its books.

A. 6. There are two conditions under which audits may be conducted, either secretly or unexpectedly, without any warning to the bookkeepers or other employees as to the time and scope of the audit, or at the close of a fiscal period after a previous announcement that it was to take place.

An audit under the circumstances first mentioned, being mainly for the purpose of detecting irregularities among the employees, it is obvious that no intimation of what is to take place should precede the auditor's visit, and he therefore enters upon his work taking the accounts in whatever condition he may find them and relying entirely upon his own methods and penetration to get upon the right track of inquiry.

A formal audit under the second conditions usually has for its object the complete review of all transactions and the investigation of all values, preparatory to certifying to the profit and loss account and balance sheet, and being strictly a review it calls for the completion beforehand of the work to be reviewed, and renders it proper for the auditor to require such matters to be in readiness and such facilities available as will aid him in the prompt and expeditious performance of his duty, viz :

All footings in the books of original entry should be confirmed in ink, all postings to the ledger made, and a trial balance taken off and agreed.

All vouchers for payments should be arranged in order and available, also all requisite or available dockets confirmatory of purchases, sales, returns or other entries susceptible of collateral proof, together with stock sheets giving full particulars of quantities and prices, duly signed by the persons who prepared them.

All deeds, mortgages, bonds, bills receivable, and all other securities and pledges should be simultaneously produced, with a list thereof in agreement with the values appearing in the ledger.

The cash book should be shut off at the close of the last day of the period under review and all cash remaining on hand should be deposited in bank; or in case of this being omitted all vouchers for subsequent payments should be ready and in order.

The auditor may further require other matters or facilities which the nature of the business or the circumstances of the audit render requisite.

Q. 7.   What evidence should be required as to the correctness of values of assets (other than customers' accounts) entered in the books?

A. 7.   In respect to some classes of assets, it would be necessary to first obtain evidence of their existence, as well as subsequently to determine their values.

As to stocks, bonds and similar properties, a personal inspection of the instruments themselves should be made and their values established by reference to published lists, or if unlisted, by sufficient evidence that the price paid or value for which they were taken was conservative and subject to no material shrinkage.

As to lands and buildings, the title deeds of the property should be examined as well as the subsequent expenditure thereon, and as to plant, machinery, etc., actual inspection, and examination of the ledger accounts for same together with vouchers for the purchases thereof, should be made, care being exercised, as to both classes of property, that no inflation of value by capitalization of purely revenue expenditure had occurred, and that sufficient outlay for maintenance and repairs and adequate depreciation had been charged to profit and loss.

As to stock-in-trade, proper inventories, signed by the persons who took same, should be required, and the extensions and additions thereof carefully gone over; in any instance where radical changes in value of any class of goods from that shown in former inventories is manifest, the matter should receive prompt inquiry before being passed.

As to good-will, patent rights, franchises, etc., a critical inquiry into the degree in which they are actual and necessary assets or constitute out-and-out loading should be fearlessly and impartially made; and in either case clear expression of the fact should be given on the balance sheet by their location either among the actual assets or ranking them against the capital and surplus.

Q. 8. State what is necessary in auditing cash payments, and how to prevent the reproduction and passing of vouchers a second time.

A. 8. The examination of all vouchers which are produced as evidence of the genuineness and propriety of payments of debts and disbursements of cash is regarded as the fundamental and most essential part of an audit, and should be carried to the utmost possible extent, thereby including not only receipted invoices or separate receipts relating thereto, but a comparison of the same with monthly statements received and cheques returned by the bank, as well as the scrutiny of signatures and endorsements thereon.

To prevent the reproduction and passing of vouchers a second time, the auditor should write the date of the voucher and his initials in plain bold characters across the face and through the material part of the voucher, in red or other colored ink, so as practically to deface the voucher and render it impossible for his audit mark to be overlooked, or removed without the erasure being apparent.

In cases where vouchers are not produced, unless the items are of trivial amounts and obviously unquestionable in character, a list thereof should be made and their admissibility established by other evidence, or the auditor should make separate report thereon and refuse to assume any responsibility regarding them.

Q. 9. State what examination should be made of the receivable book accounts of a firm or company to ascertain what accounts, if any, should be written off as bad.

A. 9. The receivable book accounts should be examined seriatim, and the following facts inquired into, viz:

That the balances are composed of certain unsettled charges, or at least that differences allowed in former settlements which should have been written off, are not brought forward and included in the balances.

That no old charges remain unsettled while those of more recent date in the same account have been collected.

That delay in the settlement of an account or any items therein has not been protracted beyond the time specified by the terms of payment, or in the event of no specific terms, for so long a period as to render realization obviously doubtful.

As a knowledge of the standing and credit of the debtor is an important factor in judging whether the account be good or bad, it is advisable for the auditor to require the assistance of some member of the firm or officer of the company familiar with the standing of the debtors and the status of their accounts to explain any idiosyncracy which the auditor may notice, and generally to aid him in determining upon their classification as to good, doubtful or bad accounts.

Reference to correspondence, credit agency reports and outside inquiry into the connections and resources of the debtor will often prove helpful in determining the disposition of doubtful accounts, and can with advantage be suggested by the auditor in cases where the amount involved is too large to admit of other than careful and extended investigation.

Q. 10. How may it be determined whether certain expenditures of a manufacturing business were of the nature of maintenance and repairs or constituted an actual betterment of the plant? State how in each case they should be dealt with in the balance sheet and in the profit and loss account.

A. 10. All expenditure which accomplishes only the replacement of worn out plant or maintains it in its efficiency without in any way increasing its value beyond the original outlay or increasing its productive power beyond what it possessed when new is comprehended in the general term of "maintenance and repairs", is properly chargeable to revenue and ranks against the income in the profit and loss account.

All expenditure which to the full extent thereof increases the original value of the plant and adds to the fullest extent of efficiency it possessed or productiveness it was capable of before such expenditure was made, constitutes an actual betterment of the plant, is properly chargeable to capital, and appears as an asset upon the balance sheet, ranking as a capital expenditure against the capital receipts of a business corporation, or opposed to the general liabilities of a firm or individual.

It frequently occurs that outlay for new plant involves both capital and revenue expenditure, as in the case of the purchase of new equipment coincidently with discarding old equipment, the old much inferior in original value to the new and yielding at sale little or no proceeds ; in such a case the capital expenditure is only to the extent of the actual betterment or the value of the new over the prime cost of the old, and (unless the value of the old has been entirely amortized by depreciation charged to the revenue of former years, admitting of the capitalization of the entire cost of the new without abatement), whatever value of the old still remains as an asset upon the books is either chargeable to revenue against the current year's income or distributable throughout several years according to the original calculations respecting the life of the equipment discarded.

Q. 11.   In auditing the accounts of a business for the first time, what books should be produced?   What would be the first duty of the auditor respecting these books?

A. 11.   In auditing the accounts of a business for the first time the auditor should call for all the books of account and subsidiary books in any wise appertaining to the period under audit, and his first duty would be to make a list or inventory of said books, giving the particulars of their labels and numbers, the names by which they are designated, the period covered by the entries contained in them, the nature of said entries if not clearly indicated by the label or title given, and the names of the clerks respectively engaged in keeping them.

There are times when this precaution is of the utmost importance, as it is thereafter impossible either to remove one book or produce another without the auditor's knowledge, such attempts simply affording a clue to the matter sought to be concealed.   As an additional precaution the auditor should stamp or initial for identification every book that he handles and inventories, as well as all important papers he has occasion to examine in the course of his audit, thus enabling him at any subsequent time to positively state whether or not any particular book or paper had been produced or withheld.

Q. 12. In auditing the accounts at the conclusion of the first fiscal year of a corporation formed to acquire an established business, what documents and records should be examined in addition to the ordinary books and subjects of an audit?

A. 12. In auditing the accounts at the conclusion of the first fiscal year of a corporation formed to acquire an established business, the auditor should examine, in addition to the ordinary books and subjects of an audit, the documents and records appertaining to the initial proceedings and transactions respecting the following matters:

The certificate of incorporation should be perused to ascertain the date thereof, the authorized capital, and the character and scope of the business to be carried on.

The contracts between the company and vendor, and the resolutions of the stockholders and directors appearing in the minute book relative thereto, should be read to determine and verify the amount of stock issued for property purchased, the basis of valuation upon which the property was taken over, the provision for working capital, and in general the quid pro quo governing the transactions with, and stock issued to, all parties identified with the promotion and formation of the company.

The subscription list, stock certificate book, transfer book and share ledger should be examined from the first share subscribed or issued up to the date of the audit, and the certificates of original issue (as distinct from subsequent transfers) should be proven to be in accord with the opening entries of capital receipts in the financial books.

The deeds or bills of sale of all realty or personalty taken over or acquired by the company and the detailed description thereof, together with any bonds or mortgages assumed or given thereon, and the minutes of the proceedings authorizing the transactions relative thereto, should be thoroughly investigated and full acquaintance therewith acquired by the auditor.

Q. 13. To what extent should an auditor hold himself responsible for the correctness of

(a) Inventories;

(b) Pay Rolls;

(c) Depreciations and Discounts?

A. 13.   An auditor should hold himself responsible for the correctness of all facts and figures coming under his investigation to the extent
that no error, oversight, or misrepresentation can be justly attributed to
any relaxation of vigilance on his part, and where circumstances do not
admit of as deep penetration as would warrant him in unconditionally
pronouncing any fact or figure as being correct, he should be explicit in
stating to what extent he had relied on presumptive evidence, in order
that his statements may not be misleading in implying a greater degree
of responsibility or certainty than he felt justified in assuming or imparting.

(a) Inventories of stock-in-trade or other properties at times admit
of a greater or lesser degree of proof respecting possession and basis of
valuation, and the auditor should avail himself of every condition, circumstance and opportunity to satisfy himself on these points ; however,
he is frequently enabled to do no more than verify the figures by checking the extensions and footings, and fasten the responsibility in all other
respects upon the parties preparing the inventories, by requiring them
to sign or swear to the same.

(b) Pay-rolls are also susceptible of audit, concerning which an
auditor may assume greater or less responsibility, conditioned upon the
thoroughness of the system and the effectiveness of the internal check
employed.   The auditor should in every instance inquire into the particulars of the time worked or work done, check the calculations and com-
pare the totals of the pay-rolls with the cash book entries.   He should
further take critical notice of the system and procedure employed in
determining and paying the wages and should call special attention to
any weak points therein or opportunities for irregularities to which it
may be exposed, and make such recommendations as will justify him in
insuring greater safety and assuming fuller responsibility in subsequent
audits.

(c) The depreciation to which the various fixed properties of almost
every class of business are subject have been repeatedly tabulated, and

many concerns have gone to considerable expense to arrive at the life of the particular properties which they possess. An auditor is therefore not destitute of resources in determining the adequacy or inadequacy of the depreciation recommended to his approval, and in the case of pronounced difference of opinion on this subject between an auditor and the directors of a company, it is incumbent upon him, if they remain obdurate, to bring the matter to the attention of the stockholders in his report, and qualify his certification of the balance sheet accordingly. In the case of firms or individuals, his responsibility extends no further than the bringing of the matter to their attention and advising them with respect thereto.

Discounts received and paid may be approximately agreed (in the absence of a detailed checking of the settlements), by comparison with the total payments to creditors and receipts from customers, respectively, in the aggregate, and the average rate per cent. that obtains ; and some such verification of the discounts respecting settlements that have transpired, as well as corresponding provisions for discounts on outstanding receivable accounts, should receive the auditor's attention.

Q. 14. In an audit stipulating for the examination of all vouchers of every description, what would be proper vouchers for the following:

Purchases,	Returned Purchases,
Sales,	Returned Sales,
Cash Receipts,	Cash Payments,

Journal Entries?

A. 14. The term "voucher" in its restricted sense as employed in accountancy signifies any document received in acknowledgement of the payment of money, or the satisfaction of a claim, that may be offered and accepted as sufficient evidence of the correctness of the entry of such fact in the accounts, and that the same is in order. It must, therefore, bear the signature, imprint or stamp of the payee, and show evidence of execution by some one, other than the party offering it in evidence. and origination from some source other than himself.

In a more comprehensive sense a voucher may be any document, record or book entry, that by reason of its appearing in chronological order or forming a part of a complete sequence, may prove circumstantially the correctness of some other entry or record made by the same person or in the accounts of the same business, and the act of vouching may imply the examination of either or both kinds of evidence, the one being the examination of receipts for cash payments, the other the tracing of sequence and confirmation thereof by means of the agreement between relative entries and records.

The receipted invoices that vouch for the payment thereof also vouch for the purchases that have been settled for, the more recent purchases remaining unliquidated being vouched by the unpaid invoices remaining on file, in either case the invoices should bear the stamp, check or mark indicating that the goods have been actually received, and should be further supported by inward freight bills, duty and custom-house charges, and warehouse ledger, or stock ledger entries where the same exist.

Return purchases may be vouched by credit memoranda received from the original vendors, confirmed by express or other transportation receipts, stock ledger entries and correspondence. The fact that the goods were first purchased should be established by reference to the original invoice and notation made thereon of such of the goods as were returned, with proper references to the books and pages on which the same were entered, both as to charge and cancellation.

Sales may be vouched by order blanks, consecutively numbered and bearing the checks and initials of the delivery clerks and others through whose hands they pass in the regular routine, or where such do not exist, by press copies or carbon duplicates of the bills following regularly in bound books, tickets signed by the customers on delivery, bills of lading, warehouse or stock book records, etc.

Return sales may be vouched by debit memoranda received from customers, correspondence, freight bills, stock ledger entries, and evidence that the goods were actually sold, by reference to the original bill with proper notations thereon of such of the goods as were received back and folio references to original credit and subsequent cancellation.

Cash receipts may be vouched by stub or counterfoil of receipt book in any business where it is customary to give a uniform receipt therefor.

by bank pass book entries, press copies of deposit slips, or any reliable class of docket that the nature of the business may afford, in additon to the credit postings in the ledger. In checking the postings of cash receipts it is customary, to work from the ledger into the cash book, to prevent ledger credits of cash receipts omitted from the cash book being checked by someone other than the auditor, who might thereby pass them over without detection.

Cash payments may be vouched by receipted invoices, separate receipts, cheques and notes returned by the bank and bearing proper endorsements, pay-rolls properly attested, requisitions coming through proper channels, and similar kinds of evidence confirmatory of the correctness of the amounts and propriety of the charges.

Journal entries may be vouched by their own manifest propriety, or if of an exceptional character, by the written consent of the parties affected (contracts or other documents), the approval of competent officials, resolutions, or special inquiry into the facts.

Q. 15. On what basis should the following assets be valued in the preparation of a balance sheet:

(a) Manufactured goods,

(b) Partially manufactured goods,

(c) Raw material,

(d) Open book accounts receivable,

(e) Stocks, bonds and other investments,

(f) Bills receivable?

A. 15. Any basis of valuation that fictitiously increases the assets in the balance sheet also fictitiously increases the profits in the revenue account, and any valuation of stock, whether raw material, partially manufactured, or in readiness for sale that *exceeds* the actual expenditure incidental to acquiring, retaining or bringing the same to its condition at the time (constituting the total outlay thereon), would result in anticipating profits depending upon future transactions. Likewise, failing to include in the valuation indirect outlay, materially contributing to actual value of stock and essentially requisite to its possession, preservation and manipulation, would result in understating both its value and the profit for the period just ended.

Raw material, of a staple nature, may command a broader market and be less subject to fluctuation in value than after manufacture into wares subject to the caprice of fashion or popular demand, which might without warning, become nearly worthless and require different treatment in valuation from what, as before stated, would normally obtain. These are considerations bearing upon particular and unusual circumstances, and vary so in an infinite variety of businesses as to preclude them from coming under any general rule, or the methods upon which values may be arrived at being specifically dealt with.

In the absence of any extraordinary shrinkages in market value beyond recovery, it is a sound principle to carry the stock at its actual cost, and let the profits or losses be determined upon final sale or disposition.

(a) Manufactured goods should therefore be valued at the prime cost of raw material, plus the freight, duty, and similar charges, labor, and a percentage of the management expenses conservatively estimated to fairly represent the extent to which they drew upon the general facilities in the various processes through which they passed.

(b) Partially manufactured goods, according to the extent that they approach completion, should be valued on the same basis as manufactured goods.

(c) Raw material should be valued at prime cost plus all subsequent direct charges for freight, duty, handling, inspecting, etc.

(d) Open book accounts receivable, should be valued at their ledger amounts, less sufficient reserve for customary discounts and estimated bad debts.

(e) Stocks, bonds, and other investments, should be valued at cost unless obviously above market quotations, in which case they should be valued at market price.

(f) Bills Receivable should be valued at face amount if good, and if bad, at nothing.

COMMERCIAL LAW.

COMMERCIAL LAW.

Q. 1. Draw the following promissory notes and forms of indorsement:

NOTES.

(a) Not negotiable;
   Maker, John Brown;
   Payee, Walter Jones;
   Amount, $1000.25;
   Time, Four months;
   Place of payment, Bank of America.
(b) Negotiable; maker, payee, amount, time and place of payment as in (a).
(c) Negotiable; requiring no indorsement.

INDORSEMENTS.

(d) Indorsement by above payee, in blank.
(e) Indorsement by above payee, to Robinson & Co. in full and further negotiable.
(f) Indorsement by Robinson & Co., relieving them from further liability.
(g) Indorsement by Robinson & Co., to Henry Miller, not further negotiable.

A. 1.

$1000\frac{25}{100}   NEW YORK, DECEMBER 16, 1896.

Four months after date I promise to pay to

WALTER JONES.....................One thousand $\frac{25}{100}$ Dollars,

at the Bank of America.

Value received.   JOHN BROWN.

(b)

$1000\frac{25}{100}   NEW YORK, DEC. 16, 1896.

Four months after date, I promise to pay to the order of

WALTER JONES....................One Thousand $\frac{25}{100}$ Dollars,

at the Bank of America.

Value received.   JOHN BROWN.

(c)

$1000\frac{25}{100}   NEW YORK, DEC. 16, 1896.

Four months after date I promise to pay to

WALTER JONES or bearer...........One Thousand $\frac{25}{100}$ Dollars,

at the Bank of America.

Value received.   JOHN BROWN.

(d)   Walter Jones.

(e)   Pay to the order of Robinson & Co.
        Walter Jones.

(f)   Without recourse.
> Robinson & Co.

(NOTE)   An indorsement "without recourse" relieves the indorser from liability only with respect to the payment of the note.   If the note or any prior indorsement is a forgery, if any of the parties to it are incompetent to make contracts, if the indorser's title is not good, or if the note has been given in violation of law and consequently is invalid, the indorser "without recourse" is liable and the holder can proceed at once against him.

(g)   Pay to Henry Miller.
> Robinson & Co.

Q. 2.   When an indorsed promissory note is not paid at maturity ;

(a) What course should the holder pursue in order to prove presentation ?

(b) Against whom can the holder bring suit for recovery ?

(c) Against whom can an indorser who has been compelled to pay this dishonored note bring suit for recovery ?

(d) Under what circumstances is an indorser relieved from liability ?

(e) How may the holder be relieved from the necessity of protesting it for non-payment ?

(f) What are the principal defenses that may be urged by the maker of a note in an action for non-payment?

(g) What defense (good as against the payee or indorser who has knowledge thereof) will not relieve the maker from liability to a subsequent purchaser in good faith before maturity ?

(h) How is the liability of indorsers affected by an agreement between the holder and the maker of the note to extend time of payment beyond maturity ?

A. 2.   (a)   The note should be immediately protested by a notary public, and a copy of the certificate of protest, and a notice of non-payment, together with a description of the note should be sent at once to the maker and each of the indorsers.

(b)   The holder can bring suit for recovery, against the maker of the note or any indorser to whom has been sent due and timely notice of its dishonor, indorsers "without recourse" excepted.

(c)   An indorser who has been compelled to pay a dishonored note, can bring suit for recovery against the maker or any prior indorser who has received due notice of non-payment.

(d)   An indorser is relieved from liability, by indorsement "without recourse," and by failure to receive due notice of non-payment through negligence on the part of the holder and transferees.

(e)   It is not necessary to protest a note for non-payment if it contains the words "no protest," "protest waived," or similar clause, or if it be expressly stipulated between the parties concerned that protest and notice of non-payment be waived ; such agreements are, however, usually, in the body of the note, and all indorsers are bound thereby.

(f)   The principal defenses that may be urged by the maker of a note in an action for non-payment, are, infancy, usury, alteration and forgery, want of consideration, and fraud or compulsion.

(g)   The defenses of want of consideration, and fraud or compulsion, are good only as between the maker and the payee, or an indorser with knowledge thereof, but a bona fide purchaser, before maturity of a note subject to such defence, can collect it from the maker.

(h)   If the holder receive money for granting an extension of the time of payment of a note, all the indorsers are forthwith discharged from liability, and the holder cannot sue them, if the maker does not pay.   In the absence of a consideration, the failure to present the note for payment at maturity, would release the indorsers at that time.

Q. 3.   Draw the following bills of exchange and forms of indorsement and acceptance :

DOMESTIC BILL.

(a) Drawer, Smith & Jones, Boston ;
    Drawee, Brown & Robinson, New York ;

Amount, $500.50 ;

Payee, Edward Hunt, New York.

Time, 10 days sight.

(b) Indorsement by payee, in blank.

(c) Acceptance by drawee, payable at Bank of New York.

FOREIGN BILL.

(d) Drawer, J. M. Wilson, Son & Co., London ;

Drawee, Flint, Heddy & Co., New York ;

Amount, $9000.50 ;

Payee, Marquand & Bro., Boston ;

Time, 60 days date.

(e) Indorsement by payee to . . . . . in full.

(f) Form of drawee's acceptance.

A. 3. (a)

$500\tfrac{50}{100}   BOSTON, MASS. DECEMBER 16, 1896.

At ten days sight pay to the order of

EDWARD HUNT.....................Five Hundred $\tfrac{50}{100}$ Dollars,

and charge to account of

SMITH & JONES.

To BROWN & ROBINSON,

NEW YORK.

(b) Edward Hunt.

(c) Accepted, Dec. 17, 1896,

payable at Bank of New York,

Brown & Robinson.

(d)

9000\frac{50}{100}$ LONDON, DEC. 1, 1896.

       Sixty days after date of this first of exchange
(second and third of same date and tenor unpaid),
pay to the order of MARQUAND & BRO., of Boston,
Nine Thousand $\frac{50}{100}$ Dollars...............................
and charge the same to account of

                                    J. M. WILSON, SON & CO.

To FLINT, HEDDY & Co.,
    NEW YORK, U. S. A.

    (e)   Pay to the order of . . . .
            Marquand & Bro.
    (f)   Accepted, Dec. 16, 1896.
            Flint, Heddy & Co.

NOTE. Indorsements are written across the back of the Bill in black ink; Acceptances are written across the face of the Bill in red ink.

The foregoing bill is one of a set of three, the other two reading respectively, "this second of exchange, (first and third of same date and tenor unpaid,)" "this third of exchange, (first and second of same date and tenor unpaid)." In many instances foreign bills are now made in duplicate only.

Q. 4.   If the drawee of a draft or bill of exchange refuses to accept the same on presentation :

(a) How is the due date of the draft or bill affected?

(b) In what manner, if any, is he liable under the draft, or bill, if he has funds of the drawer or is indebted to the drawer?

(c) On what grounds can the holder commence action?

(d) How can a third party prevent the bill from becoming due at once, and what would be his position if obliged to pay the bill?

A. 4. (a) If the drawee of a draft or bill refuses to accept the same on presentation, it becomes due at once, and the holder can immediately demand payment of the drawer.

(b) The drawee is not liable to the holder of a bill until he has accepted it, nor can the holder sue him for refusal to accept; but the drawee is liable to the drawer if he refuses to accept when in possession of funds belonging to the drawer, who can sue him for actual damages sustained.

(c) A bill before its acceptance is a contract between the drawer and the payee, and if the drawee refuses to accept the bill, or having accepted, defaults in payment, the payee by duly notifying the drawer of the facts, can sustain an action to compel him to pay it.

(d) When a bill is presented and the drawee refuses to accept it, a friend of the drawer may accept for his honor and so prevent the bill from immediately becoming due. Such acceptance is called "Acceptance supra protest," and the acceptor being an accommodation acceptor, if required to pay the bill, could claim repayment from the drawer.

Q. 5. What is a *Corporation*, and how does it differ from a joint stock company?

A. 5. A coporation consists of one or more individuals, under a grant or privilege that secures succession of members without changing the identity of the body which is described and legally regarded as one artificial person capable of transacting prescribed kinds of business the same as a natural person.

A joint stock company is of the nature of a partnership, but similar to a corporation in form, inasmuch as its capital stock is fixed in amount, divided into shares, and can be transferred, the business is conducted by officers, and the company is not dissolved by the death of a member or by sale or transfer of his stock. It is not, however, legally regarded as one artificial person and the members of such a company are individually liable as in a partnership.

Q. 6. Describe briefly the following:

(a) A sole corporation.

(b) A corporation aggregate.

(c) An eleemosynary corporation.

(d) A public corporation.

(e) A private corporation.

A. 6. (a) A sole corporation consists of a single individual who possesses corporate powers. In this country we have no sole corporations, but in England the sovereign, the bishops of the established church, and some other functionaries, each constitute a sole corporation, because each office requires a direct succession from one holder to another in order that the property belonging to the office may remain in its possession without administration by executors or administrators.

(b) A corporation aggregate consists of several individuals united in one body and may be either religious or lay, the former sometimes called ecclesiastical, are those formed for the purpose of administering the property of churches and congregations, the latter includes all other corporations both eleemosynary and civil, civil corporations being further divided into public and private.

(c) Eleemosynary corporations are those formed for charitable purposes, such as hospitals, asylums, and kindred institutions. The name is derived from eleemosyna, meaning alms.

(d) Public corporations are those created for the purpose of local government, and are given the power to legislate within certain limits subject to the control of the state legislature. Counties, cities and towns are public corporations possessing power to hold property and to sue and be sued in their corporate capacity, but differing in some respects from corporations as generally understood, they are called quasi corporations.

(e) Private corporations are those organized for private enterprise. Industrial corporations, engaged in the production, purchase, manufacture and sale of staple commodities or patented articles, as well as banks, insurance companies, and railroads, doing business of a public nature are types of private corporations.

Q. 7. Answer briefly :

(a) How may corporations be created ?

(b) What acts of a corporation are called *ultra vires ?*

(c) What is a *franchise ?*

(d) Through whom does a corporation act in transacting its business ?

(e) By whom must all contracts, deeds, mortgages, leases and other instruments binding a corporation be signed, and whence do the signers derive their authority ?

(f) Explain the manner of issuing and of transferring the capital stock of a corporation, and state the principal rights acquired by stockholders.

(g) What is the limit of a stockholder's liability ?

(h) How may a corporation be dissolved ?

A. 7. (a) Corporations are created by the State, either by charter, which is an express act of the legislature, or under general statute, by compliance with general laws providing for the formation of corporations, which laws, similar as far as the main provisions are concerned, have been enacted by the legislatures of most if not all of the states and territories. Public corporations, except in a few of the states, are created by charter, while private corporations are organized under general statutes.

(b) Any act of a corporation beyond the power conferred upon it by its charter or the general law under which it was created is called "*ultra vires.*"

(c) A franchise is a particular right, privilege or immunity, generally exclusive in its nature, conferred by grant from a sovereign or a government, and vested in individuals or corporations. The franchise of a railroad is the right to operate its road and has a value separate and distinct from that of the plant or ordinary property, and in some instances the franchise of a corporation may not be sold except by consent of the conferring power.

(d) Corporations act through their officers, (the president, secretary, treasurer and board of directors or trustees,) who are appointed or elected by the stockholders. A majority of the directors control, and the stockholders, beyond the power of electing the officers, usually have no further concern in the transactions of the corporate business.

(e) The president must sign all contracts, deeds, mortgages, leases, and other instruments binding the corporation, and often the signature of the secretary is required as well. The signers derive their authority from the board of directors whose consent is expressed by resolution and vote. The seal of the corporation should be affixed.

(f) The capital stock is divided into shares of specified value, and one or more certificates are issued to each stockholder, representing the number of shares of capital stock to which he is entitled. Shares of stock are personal property and may be sold and transferred, but in order that the transferee may acquire the privileges of a stockholder, the transfer must be made upon the books of the company. To do this the transferor executes a bill of sale and power of attorney authorizing the transfer for which a form is printed on the back of the certificate. The certificate thus indorsed is presented to the proper officer of the corporation who thereupon cancels it and preserves it for future reference, and issues a new certificate for a like amount to the new holder of the stock, after making the proper transfer entries on the books.

The principal rights of stockholders are as follows :

To vote in person or by proxy at meetings held for the purpose of electing the officers, each stockholder having as many votes as he has shares, so that a holder or holders of the majority of the shares may elect all of the officers.

To participate in the profits out of which dividends are declared and in the assets upon dissolution of the corporation, each stockholder participating in the proportion that the amount of his stock bears to the whole of the stock of the same class.

A stockholder may obtain an injunction to restrain the president or directors from acting in a manner injurious to the corporation, and may hold them liable for bad faith in the use of its funds.

(g) The stockholders of a corporation are usually not liable for the debts of the company beyond the amount of the stock held by them, and in the event of the corporation becoming bankrupt they lose only their investment by reason of the stock becoming worthless. The holders of national bank stock are liable to double the amount of the face value of their stock and in case of the failure of the bank, each stockholder, in addition to the loss of his stock, is to the amount of his stock personally liable for the corporate debts and may be assessed accordingly. In some of the states modifications have been made increasing the stockholders' liability, in particular cases, to an individual liability for all the debts of the corporation; but in general the liability is lim-ited to the loss of stock only, or to both the loss of stock and an addi-tional liability equal thereto.

(h) Public corporations may be dissolved by the legislature. A private corporation may be dissolved by the expiration of the period limited in its charter, by consent of stockholders and surrender of franchise, by forfeiture of its franchise, (caused by wrong use, called "mis-user," or by failure to use, called "non-user,") under a court decree upon an action brought by the Attorney-General in a proceeding called a "quo warranto," and in some states by an action instituted by a judg-ment creditor. Upon the dissolution of a corporation it is usual for the court to appoint a receiver to take charge of its property, pay its debts, and wind up its affairs.

Q. 8. Answer briefly :

(a) What is a *contract?*

(b) How is a contract made ?

(c) What are some kinds of contracts which must be in writing ?

(d) What are some forms of contracts which must be under seal?

(e) Which contracts if made on Sunday are void, and which are not void ?

A. 8. (a) A contract is an agreement, based upon a cause or consid-eration between two or more persons, to do, or to abstain from doing, some particular act or thing. An agreement without a consideration, or the promise of one person to do, or not to do, some particular thing gratuitously and without obligation on the part of another, is not a con-tract and cannot be enforced.

(b) A contract is made orally, in writing, or in writing under seal, by competent persons, who understand the subject, matter or thing contracted about and mutually enter into an agreement with respect thereto for consideration or inducement promised or offered.

(c) The following kinds of contracts must be in writing: Contracts for the sale of land; leases for more than one year; marriage settlements;

guarantees or promises to pay the debt of another, if he does not; contracts which require more than one year for execution; contracts for the sale of goods of the value of fifty dollars or upwards. Other kinds of contracts are frequently put in writing for the purpose of avoiding controversy.

(d) Deeds, mortgages, leases, and all instruments concerning real estate, as well as bonds and other agreements involving important interests, are forms of contracts which require a seal to be attached, and are called "contracts of specialty". In some states an actual wax or paper seal is requisite, in the greater number of states a scroll made with a pen is sufficient, while in many of the Western States the seal is understood and no actual seal or mark indicative thereof is necessary to make valid some contracts of specialty.

(e) All contracts made on Sunday, as a general rule, are void, except contracts which concern what are known as works of mercy or necessity, as for the providing of food or medicine in cases of emergency or for the performance of services under unavoidable physical conditions which would entail serious loss or injury if deferred. In some states, however, statutes forbid entering into any contract on Sunday, no matter of what nature or under what circumstances; nevertheless, there is a growing tendency on the part of the courts to regard such matters according to their merits.

Q. 9. Answer briefly:

(a) What is a *debt* and what can a creditor demand in payment of a debt?

(b) When a creditor accepts in satisfaction payment of less than the full amount of a debt, how can the debtor guard against further demands?

(c) When, where and to whom must payment of a debt be made?

(d) Is the debtor legally entitled to a receipt?

(e) Which has the prior right to apply a payment against any one of several debts, the debtor or the creditor?

(f) When a partial payment is made on a debt bearing interest, in what manner is it applied?

(g) When does the period of limitation begin to run, and what are some of the ways in which its operation can be modified?

A. 9 (a) A debt is a matured obligation of one party, called a debtor, to pay a certain sum of money to another party, called a creditor, for value received. When a verdict is given and judgment rendered for a certain sum, the obligor becomes a judgment debtor. A creditor can demand in payment of a debt, legal tender money, which includes gold and silver coin, United States treasury notes, subsidiary silver coin to an amount not exceeding ten dollars, and nickel and copper coin to an amount not exceeding twenty-five cents. Bank notes, gold and silver certificates issued prior to 1890, and foreign money, are not legal tender.

(b) Payment of less tnan the full amount, even when the creditor promises to forgive the balance, does not extinguish a debt, as there is no consideration for the promise; if, however, in addition to the part payment, or without it, the creditor accepts in full satisfaction something other than money or that which is claimed, no matter how slight its value, the debt is discharged by what is called "an accord and satisfaction." A most effective method of securing the debtor against further demands is for him to get the creditor to execute a release under seal, which, being a contract of specialty, implies a consideration.

(c) Payment of a debt must be made on the day when it falls due, or if not paid will bear interest from that day until paid. If any place be specified, payment must be made at that place, or, if no place be mentioned, payment must be made at the creditor's office, or residence, or wherever he may be, the debtor being required to find his creditor, and not the creditor to seek the debtor. Payment must be made to the creditor personally, or to his agent or representative who is obviously authorized, or by usage of his business accustomed to receive it.

(d) A receipt is a matter of courtesy on the part of the creditor, and the debtor at the time of paying the debt cannot demand one. It is customary, however, for the creditor to give a receipt; but if he refuses, to do so, the only remedy for the debtor is to have a witness to the payment.

(e) The debtor has the prior right to apply a payment against any of several debts, and if he directs the creditor to cancel a particular debt therewith, the creditor must do so; but if the debtor specifies no application of the payment, the creditor may apply it to any of the debts.

(f) A partial payment made on a debt bearing interest is first applied in payment of interest, and if more than sufficient, the remainder is applied in payment of principal.

(g) The period of limitation begins when the debt becomes due and the creditor has a right to sue. Commencement of action and service of a summons upon the debtor, even on the last day of the period of limitation, saves all the rights of the creditor, who can recover his claim or a judgment at any time he chooses to press the suit. An acknowledgment of the debt and a promise to pay it in writing by the debtor within the period or afterwards, revives the debt and makes it good again for the legal period commencing from the new promise, and a part payment by the debtor, whether of interest or principal, has the same effect.

If the creditor is not in the state when the debt becomes due, the period of limitation does not run until he comes or returns into the state, and if the creditor never comes into the state, the debt is never outlawed. If the debtor is not in the state the period does not run until he enters it, and if he departs again, the time he is absent is not counted, and the debt is not outlawed until the sum of the various periods during which the debtor has been in the state amounts in all to the legal period.

Q. 10. What is a *partnership?* How may the relationship of partner be established? Define *nominal partner, silent partner, dormant partner, special partner.*

A. 10. A partnership is the relationship resulting from a compact between two or more competent persons for combining their money, goods, labor and skill, or any or all of them, for the purpose of undertaking or prosecuting any lawful adventure, trade or business, with the understanding that they shall share in the profits and losses. This relationship may be established by a written contract under seal, or not under seal, by verbal agreement, or by implication, the test of a partnership being a community of interest and the right to a voice in the direction of its affairs. Partners collectively are referred to as a house or firm.

A nominal partner is one who allows his name to appear in the firm name, or represents himself as a member of the firm when in reality he has no interest in or control of its affairs; but to the extent that the firm receives credit by such representations he is liable for its debts.

A silent partner is one whose name does not appear in the firm name, and who while having an interest in the firm and a voice in the direction of its affairs, does not so represent himself in order to avoid the responsibility of an ostensible partner; he is liable, however, to the fullest extent whenever his relationship becomes known.

A dormant partner is one who invests capital but takes no part in controlling or directing the affairs of the firm. He may be either an ostensible or a silent partner, but the term is commonly interchangable with silent or secret partner.

A special partner is one of the partners in a limited partnership, whose liability for the debts of the firm is limited to the amount of capital he has invested. He has no right to actively manage the affairs of the firm, and should he do so, can be held liable as a general partner.

Q. 11. In what respects are partners trustees for each other, and in what respects are they agents for each other?

A. 11. Partners are trustees for each other as between themselves, and everything they do must inure to the benefit of the firm. No partner can take advantage of his position as partner for private gain, and if he, without the knowledge of the other partners, conducts a separate business to which the firm name or credit in any wise contributes, the other partners have a right to claim a pro rata share of the profits therefrom.

Partners are agents for each other as to transactions with third parties, and each partner has power to bind the firm by his acts if within the scope of the partnership business.

Q. 12. What are the relative liabilities of a new partner and a retiring partner?

A. 12. A new partner on coming into the firm is not responsible for the debts of the old firm, unless he expressly assumes them; he is, however, liable for the debts of the firm incurred subsequently to his becoming a member.

A partner on retiring from a firm, if he neglects to give notice of the fact by publication and private advices to all persons who might otherwise continue dealing with the firm under the impression that he was still a member, is liable for the debts of the firm, in the event of a failure, to all such persons, the same as a nominal partner.

Q. 13. How is a limited partnership formed?

A. 13. A limited partnership is formed in pursuance of a statute authorizing such, and in those states only where special statutes allowing the formation of limited partnerships have been enacted. The persons forming such a partnership are required to make, sign, and execute a certificate, which is filed with the public records of the state and county in which the business is to be transacted, and states the name of the firm, the nature of its business, together with the names of the general and special partners, and the amount of capital contributed by each. In some states it is necessary to publish in the newspapers for a certain time the terms of the partnership.

Q. 14. State the difference between a sale and a consignment.

A. 14. A sale is the transfer of property, or the title thereto, from one person to another, for a price in money, paid or to be paid. The only requisites being the promise to deliver on the part of the vendor and the promise to pay therefor on the part of the vendee, for the latter to acquire title to personal property.

A consignment is the delivery or commitment of goods in trust by one party to another for superintendence or sale, the consignee acting and accounting as factor, agent, and trustee for the consignor, in whom the title to the goods remains vested until lawfully acquired by third parties.

Q. 15. What kind of action can the consignor maintain against a consignee who converts to his own use the proceeds of the sale of consignor's goods?

A. 15. A consignee who converts to his own use the proceeds of the sale of his consignor's goods, is not only in default with respect to his accounting, but is guilty of embezzlement, and therefore renders his person as well as his estate liable, and the consignor can institute and maintain, or cause to be instituted and maintained, either a civil or a criminal action, or both, against the consignee, at one and the same time.

BALANCE SHEETS.

BALANCE SHEETS.

A Balance Sheet implies more than a Statement of Assets and Liabilities, for while the latter term is the more proper title under which the resources and obligations of a business conducting its accounts by single-entry or crude memoranda might be compiled, a Balance Sheet presupposes by its very name the existence of accounts kept by double-entry, and its origin from a Trial Balance of a ledger in perfect equilibrium containing a revenue account in explanation of the item of surplus or deficit appearing on the Balance Sheet as well as accounts of all the items of assets and liabilities also appearing thereon.

A Balance Sheet is, therefore, a concise statement abstracted from a ledger in perfect balance, whereas a Statement of Assets and Liabilities, although dealing with the same subjects, may be compiled from any data obtainable, no matter how crude or miscellaneous.

In the preparation of Balance Sheets, three general forms are in use, the technical form, the report form, and the working-paper form.

The technical form is distinguished by the assets appearing on one side and the liabilities on the other, and being the main subject under consideration will hereinafter be dealt with at length.

The report form is one adopted for convenience, where a Balance Sheet occurs in the body of a report, or is published in the newspapers, or wherever it is inconvenient to give it the breadth required by the technical form, and the assets are accordingly stated first and the liabilities after and under, the assets topping the liabilities, in a single column.

The working-paper form is almost exclusively to be found in American text books on book-keeping, in use in the various business colleges and commercial schools.

It consists of a trial balance in the ordinary form, having the names of the accounts in a perpendicular column, to the right of which is a double (Dr. and Cr.) money column containing the debit and credit balances of the accounts, which money columns are immediately followed by a series of like double (Dr. and Cr.) money columns.

The nominal accounts on the trial balance representing elements of profit and loss are each extended (by repeating the figures) into the next pair of columns which are headed "Loss and Gain."

The capital accounts are, in like manner, each extended into further and separate pairs of columns headed respectively with the names of the proprietors, to which is also carried the proportion of the balance of the "Loss and Gain" columns representing the net profit or loss appertaining to each, after which the capital columns are each balanced and the balances together with the real accounts, on the trial balance, representing assets and liabilities, are extended into the next succeeding and last pair of columns which are headed "Resources and Liabilities."

While this form affords an excellent illustration of the process of roughly analysing a trial balance preparatory to framing a balance sheet and a revenue account, it is but a working-paper and incapable of giving the adequate expression to the complicated articulation and relation of values called for in a Balance Sheet suitable for presentation as a financial statement. It is only because of the fact that the works in which it appears hold it out to the student as *the* form of balance sheet, and it consequently (although seldom) appears under such title as a finished statement, that any notice whatsoever is given to it in this work, as from an accountancy standpoint it is valueless, its manifest limitations not admitting of its use even as a working paper. It can therefore be only regarded as a somewhat neat, school-room exercise, and that, no doubt, is all its originator intended it should be.

The technical balance sheet has been the subject of much study and debate, and views, concerning its form and expression, at once radically different and conflicting confront us at the outset.

The advent of English Chartered Accountants to the United States and other countries, occasioned by the extensive investment of English capital in those countries, and the consequent commission of English accountants to guard the interests represented, has resulted in so wide a dissemination of the English form of balance sheet that it is necessary to make thorough inquiry into its distinctive features, more especially as it is at variance and in direct conflict with the technical form of balance sheet used throughout the rest of the world.·

Many of the leading English Chartered Accountants are opposed to the English form, and have clearly expressed their preference for the Continental form of balance sheet used throughout Europe and the United States, but in deference to their established usage, further confirmed by "The Companies' Act, 1862, 25 and 26 Vict., c. 89," and "the Life Assurance Act, 1870, 33 and 34 Vict. c. 61." All opposition among chartered accountants to their prevailing form of balance sheet seems to have subsided. At the same time there fortunately appears to be strong inclination on the part of accountants in other countries to adhere to the Continental form.

No better insight into the merits of the case can be had than by a brief review of what English Chartered Accountants themselves have had to say on the subject.

On 20th October, 1882, a paper was read before the Manchester Society of Chartered Accountants, by Mr. Edwin Guthrie, F. C. A., on "The want of uniformity in the modes of stating accounts;" and while he treated chiefly with the variety of titles in use as headings to published revenue accounts of Insurance companies, he also drew attention to the difference between the present English form of balance sheet in which the assets are shown on the right-hand or credit side contra to the liabilities on the left-hand or debit side, and the Continental form, in which the assets are shown on the left-hand or debit side contra to the liabilities on the right-hand or credit side, the same as in the ledger; declaring his preference for the latter form, and submitting in support of its orthodoxy the following works on book-keeping, (see page 86) in which, out of eleven works dating from 1721 to 1865 only two, of comparatively recent date, show a preference for the English form,

BALANCE SHEETS.

MODE OF PLACING ASSETS AND LIABILITIES IN BALANCE SHEETS,
As Adopted by some of English Authors of Works on Book-keeping.

Author.	Date.	Title.	Modes of Placing.		
William Webster,	1721	Essay on Book-keeping,	Balance "Dr." (Debts due to me.)		(Debts owing Cr. by me.)
Chas. Hutton, LL.D.F.R.S	1810	A Complete Treatise on Book-keeping,	Balance,	Assets.	Liabilities.
Rees Cyclopedia,	1819	Article on Book-keeping,	Balance,	Assets.	Liabilities.
James Morrison,	1825	The Elements of Book-keeping	Balance,	Assets.	Liabilities.
C. Morrison,	1834	A Complete System of Practical Book-keeping,	Balance Account, Assets.		Liabilities.
Isaac Preston Corg	1839	Practical Treatise on Accounts	Balance Account, Assets.		Liabilities.
J. Caldecott,	1850	Practical Guide to Book-keeping,	Balance Account, Assets.		Liabilities.
B. F. Foster,	1852	Double Entry Elucidated,	Balance Sheet, Assets,		Liabilities.
W. Inglis,	1858	Book-keeping,	Balance Sheet, Liabilities.		Assets.
With a remark that in some systems the Balance Sheet is Dr. Assets, Cr. Liabilities, the position being reversed.					
James Haddon,	1859	Rudimentary Book-keeping.	Balance Account, Assets.		Liabilities.
R. S. E. Farries,	1865	Joint Stock Companies,	Balance Sheet, Liabilities.		Assets.

After discussing both revenue accounts and balance sheets and commenting upon copies of published accounts which he submitted, Mr. Guthrie states :

"It will be noticed that I have almost wholly omitted the use of the terms 'Debit' and 'Credit,' in favor of the somewhat awkward terms, 'Left-hand side ' and 'Right-hand side.' I have done so because in the face of the confusion of positions to which the various elements of accounts are assigned, the former terms—most useful in their true application—have in final statements, come to mean little, if anything, more than left and right respectively.   *   *   *   *   As the consideration of the question immediately dealt with was one of mere *sides*, and so far as I propose to deal with Balance Sheets, the question is one of sides also; I propose to bring Balance Sheets into review at this point, and to consider other forms and questions of account afterwards. The question at this point then is—on which side should the assets appear on a Balance Sheet, and consequently on which side the Liabilities? Many English accountants to whom I have put the question have answered without hesitation—the Liabilities on the Left the Assets on the Right, and with this dismiss the question as beyond controversy. Nevertheless the alternative answer is given by qualified English accountants, and it is a notable fact that the reverse form is almost, if not quite, universal in all foreign countries. Thus the practice which is common throughout the rest of the world is singular in England.

"It is also a fact, no less notable, that up to quite recent years, all works on Book-keeping exhibit under the term "Balance" or "Balance Account," Assets on the Left and Liabilities on the Right hand side; that English works on Book-keeping now in print and in use display their Balance Sheets in reverse of each other, thus: the two books used as the text books of the Society of Arts (Hamilton and Ball, and that of the Rev. J. Hunter, instructor of candidates for the Civil Service and other public examinations) are in reverse of each other, the former being in the popular form and the latter in the form which is exceptional in England but otherwise almost universal.

"Appended is a list of English works on Book-keeping to which I have referred, by which it would appear that the greater number of authorities give the true practice as the reverse of that popularly practiced in this country. (See page 86.)

For further illustration, if such be needed, of the anomalies of practice in this respect, it is within my knowledge that the several partners in English firms of Chartered Accountants issue Balance Sheets stated in forms the reverse of each other. Thus as this disunity of practice does exist, the requisition that one form should be established as common is a reasonable one, and the question is repeated: "Which is the proper one ?

"In seeking the answer, I put to myself one or two preliminary questions. What is the occasion and purpose of the Statement? The drawing of the Statement arises out of the requirements to know the balances on a given ledger. If the whole contents of the ledger could be seen and comprehended at one view, the requisition for the presentation of a Balance Sheet would not be made, for it would be unnecessary. To bring the balances of the ledger into one view it is necessary that the balances should be marshalled and condensed into a few lines. This is, in fact, what a Balance Sheet is and what a Balance Sheet should always be.

"Why, in the process of condensation, the balance should change sides, is for someone else to explain, I cannot.

"I have heard it contended that a Balance Sheet is a personal account made out as against the proprietor of any given Ledger. To set up this fiction is at least gratuitous. A Balance Sheet is the balance of the Ledger—the balance of the proprietor of the Ledger. I claim it is not an account at all.

"On the question of convenience, I do not lose sight of the fact that some temporary annoyance would be involved in making the change from the present popular form of Balance Sheet, to the less used, and, as I consider, proper form; but the trouble would be transitory, and would be as nothing compared to the relief afforded to the public at large from the establishment of consistent and uniform practices.

"It is clear also that unless any changes deemed desirable were promulgated with something like authority, they would not be likely to be generally carried out, especially as certain accounts in the form herein condemned as contrary to true principles are settled by Act of Parliament or orders in council, as for instance: * * * * The form of Balance Sheet settled under Table A of the Companies' Act and for Life Insurance Companies' Accounts." * * * * * * * * * * * * * *

In the next month a debate was had on Mr. Guthrie's paper, which was concluded by a unanimous resolution. "That it is desirable that the accounts of joint stock companies and public bodies be stated in a uniform manner, which should be compulsory."

Considerable correspondence followed confined chiefly to the subject of the Balance Sheet, and appearing in the columns of "The Accountant," (the official organ of Chartered Accountants throughout the world), three of which communications we reproduce as serving in concise form to illustrate the point at issue."

"THE WANT OF UNIFORMITY IN ACCOUNTS.

"MANCHESTER, November 8, 1892.
"*To the Editor of the "Accountant."*

"Sir:—Referring to the report of Mr. Guthrie's lecture at Manchester and the debate which followed, there are one or two points which I shall be glad to draw attention to.

"A great deal was said about the mode of stating balance sheets, and a proposal was made for the reversal of the ordinary practice, which is to enumerate the liabilities on the debit side and the assets on the credit side of the statement, the lecturer saying that he could not explain why the balance was transposed on being carried to the balance sheet.

"I am glad to see that the proposal was resisted by several speakers, and since the matter has been brought before the profession it seems desirable that there should be a clear expression of opinion on it.

"I think it is impossible to maintain that the balance sheet is merely a condensed list of balances, but assert on the contrary that it is a statement of the composition of the capital account of the concern to which it relates. It is the correct practice, I believe, with accountants to head the balance sheet with the name of the estate, and preface the enumeration of the liabilities and assets with the words ' To' and ' By.' This would be nonsense if the liabilities and assets were reversed, but is intelligible enough according to the present practice.

" The business is debtor to the parties to whom it owes money and creditor by the amount of its property, the balance sheet being the explanation of the balance on capital account. * * * * *

Yours, etc.,   W."

"WANT OF UNIFORMITY IN ACCOUNTS.

"2 Clarence Building, Booth Street,

" MANCHESTER, 14th November, 1882.

"*To the Editor of the "Accountant."*

"Sir:—In your issue of last week W.refers to two positions taken by me in my recent paper on ' The Want of Uniformity in the Modes of Stating Accounts.' The first point is in relation to the proper sides upon which to state the assets and liabilities respectively in a balance sheet, the second point as to the identity of profit and loss, and revenue accounts.

"To give an answer to W. is, I fear, but to repeat the arguments in my paper, which are to the effect that a balance sheet is a statement of the ledger, of a person by himself, for himself; or of a firm by themselves, for themselves; or of a company, by the officers of the company, for the proprietors of the company. This is the actual fact, and it is the logic of FACT with which we have to deal ; whereas modern English usage has accustomed W. and the majority to assumption of a fiction, the fiction that the balance sheet is a personal account with the implied heading 'A. B. in account with the World,' the World being the renderers of the account.

"If the balance sheet could be properly treated as an account at all— a personal account—the true implied heading would be ' The World in account with A. B.,' for A. B. is the renderer of the account; indeed, the only one capable of rendering it. This necessarily throws the assets on the left and the liabilities on the right hand side, and would justify the 'To' and 'By' in those respective positions. * * * * * * * *

Yours, etc.,   Edwin Guthrie."

"32 Brown Street,

"MANCHESTER, 16th November, 1882.

"To the Editor of the "Accountant."

"Sir:—Permit me to say a word on this subject. In my humble judgment the debate which followed Mr. Guthrie's able lecture was not worthy of our profession.

"I submit that to put the Liabilities on the Dr. side of a Balance Sheet is an obvious violation of the principles of book-keeping—principles that are fixed, and do not admit of opinion.

"All statements of account are, or ought to be, extracts or abstracts from the books; hence, the person to whom a statement is rendered, is always theoretically the Dr. of the account just as it stands in the ledger. A limited liability company renders a (statement) balance sheet to the shareholders; how can the shareholders be Dr. for their subscribed capital?

*   *   *   *   *   *   *   *   *   *   *   *   *

"The statement of assets and liabilities may or may not be considered a complete balance sheet in itself, but it is usually accompanied at least with a profit and loss account. In such cases, whether condensed or not, the profit and loss account consists of a portion of the ledger balances, whilst the assets and liabilities comprise the remainder, and both together embrace the whole of the ledger balances. The profit and loss part of the abstracted balance is admitted to be in proper form when taken from the ledger as it stands there; then why not the remainder, which is the assets and liabilities?

"I maintain that a correct balance sheet can be nothing more nor less than an abstract from the books, to be consistent with its name.

Yours, etc.,   C. O. N."

As a final expression of sentiment indicative of the feeling of hopeless resignation to the inevitable and general confusion in the minds of students brought about by the adoption of the English form of balance sheet, we quote question and answer No. 3, given at the Special Final Examination of the Institute of Chartered Accountants, March, 1887, appearing on page 5, section F, of "The Accountants' Manual," Vol. I, published by Gee & Co., London, which reads as follows:

"Q. 3.   In taking over a business, what account is it that exhibits solvency or insolvency? On which side of the said accounts are the Assets and Liabilities respectively placed?"

"A. 3.   A balance sheet, if the books are kept by double entry, or a statement of assets and liabilities if they are kept by single entry. Neither, however, could be correctly described as an *account*. The sides upon which assets and liabilities respectively should be placed is a debatable question, and as Members of the Council of the Institute of Chartered Accountants, expressly disagree on the matter, any expression of opinion given here is subject to their better judgment whenever they can come to a unanimous conclusion. The most prevalent practice is for assets to be placed on the right hand or credit side, and liabilities on the left hand or debit side. The form of balance sheet prescribed by Table A is drawn up on this plan. So also is the form prescribed by the Life Assurance Companies' Acts. The Institute of Chartered Accountants makes up its balance sheet on the same lines. There is, in fact, a general consensus of opinion that liabilities' on he left, assets on the right hand side, is the better plan; it has, undoubtedly, a great balance of authority in its favor; and apart altogether from the advantage of securing uniformity and the great inconvenience of departing from well established usages, the writer is disposed to think that the popular form is strictly correct."

From the foregoing papers, culminating in the somewhat satirical answer just quoted, it is obvious that the advocates of the Continental form of Balance Sheet, in which the assets and liabilities are respectively enumerated on the same si.es as they appear in the ledger, have theoretically the better of the argument, and the concurrence of the civilized world, barring England.

The advocates of the English form, however, seem to have stolen a march upon their opponents and effected the crystalization and adoption of their preference in the matter by means of The Companies' Act of 1862, and the Insurance Companies' Act of 1870, and other Acts of Parliament, thereby placing the whole body of Chartered Accountants, with respect to the form of balance sheet, in a fix, from which it seems they cannot extricate themselves.

As the advocates of untenable theories are notoriously the most stubborn, there is little doubt but that for years to come the English will adhere to their form of balance sheet as tenaciously as to their £, s and d, while the rest of the world will go on using a balance sheet requiring no metaphysical argument to support its premises, and enjoy the convenience thereof, as they also enjoy the convenience of their decimal currencies.

Another point, suggested by the form of balance sheet prescribed by Table A, to which frequent allusions have been made, is the arrangement of the assets and liabilities, that is, the order in which they follow one another, and besides being a subject in itself worthy of consideration, it will shed considerable light on the probable cause of the origination of the English form.

In order to better illustrate the subject about to be treated with we present the form of balance sheet prescribed by Table A (see page 93).

The earliest conception of accounts related to those of a steward, the fiduciary accounting of the servants and bailiffs to the lord of the manor, in which they charged themselves with that which was entrusted to them and the increase thereof, and credited themselves with what was consumed or expended in the execution of their trust, finally accounting to their lord for the balance remaining in their possession.

This theme has characterized all "judiciary" accountings under the direction of the courts, and to the present day the accounts of trustees, executors, administrators, guardians, and public officials partake of the simple form of a cash account, wherein they are charged with what they

Form prescribed by Table A, Company's Acct, 1862.

| DR. | BALANCE SHEET OF THE | CO., MADE UP TO | 18 | CR. |

Capital and Liabilities.	£ s d	£ s d	Property and Assets.	£ s d	£ s d
I. Capital. Showing: 1. The number of shares 2. The amount paid per share 3. If any arrears of calls, the nature of the arrears and the names of the defaulters 4. The particulars of any forfeited shares			**III. Property held by the Company.** Showing: 7. Immovable property, distinguishing: (a) Freehold land (b) " buildings (c) Leasehold " 8. Movable property, distinguishing: (d) Stock in trade (e) Plant The cost to be stated with deductions for deteriorations in value as charged to the reserve fund or profit and loss.		
II. Debts and Liabilities of the Company Showing: 5. The amount of loans on mortgages or debenture bonds 6. The amount of debts owing by the Company, distinguishing: (a) Debts for which acceptances have been given (b) Debts to tradesmen for supplies of stock in trade or other articles (c) Debts for law expenses (d) Debts for interest on debentures or other loans (e) Unclaimed dividends (f) Debts not enumerated above			**IV. Debts owing to the Company.** Showing: 9. Debts considered good for which the Company holds bills or other securities 10. Debts considered good for which the Company holds no securities 11. Debts considered doubtful and bad Any debt due from a director or other officer of the Company to be separately stated		
VI. Reserve Fund. Showing: The amount set aside from profits to meet contingencies			**V. Cash and Investments.** Showing: 12. The nature of investment and rate of interest 13. The amount of cash where lodged and if bearing interest		
VII. Profit and Loss. Showing: The disposable balance for payment of dividend, &c.					
Contingent Liabilities. Claims against the Company not acknowledged as debts Monies for which the Company is contingently liable					

receive, and credited with what they pay for account of the trust imposed, and also with the balance they deliver over at the conclusion of their official life.

This conception evidently possessed the minds of the designers of the Table A form of Balance Sheet, which, if reduced to a soliloquy, would read as follows:

We, the officers (of the company), appointed to administer the estate of the stockholders, do hereby render to them an accounting of the trust imposed in us, as follows:

We Charge ourselves with—

The amount paid in by shareholders for which capital stock has been issued;

The amount of loans received on mortgages or debenture bonds;

The property that has been acquired by and services rendered to this company upon credit and for which the Company still owes, with respect to acceptances given, supplies of stock-in-trade or other articles; legal services, interest on loans, unclaimed dividends, etc.;

The amount of increase or earnings,—

Set aside to meet contingencies;

Disposable for payment of dividend, etc.;

All of which constitute the sum of the Charge.

We Credit ourselves with—

Expenditure for immovable property, to wit: land, buildings, leasehold, etc.;

Expenditure for movable property, to wit: stock-in-trade, and plant, which latter is stated with deductions for deterioration in value as charged to the reserve fund or profit and loss;

Bills Receivable, book accounts of trade creditors, considered good, and book accounts of trade creditors, considered doubtful or bad;

Investments in interest-bearing securities.

All of which constitute the sum of the Discharge, as to expenditure: the Cash remaining in our hands and lodged in bank constitutes the

Balance, which, together with the foregoing expenditures, completes the Discharge.

While in the fiduciary form of account the foregoing statement would assume the report form, and the assets, representing expenditure, would be deducted from the liabilities, representing receipts, and show a remainder equivalent to the cash on hand, the placing of the liabilities on the debit side and the assets on the credit side (under a like construction of the purpose of the statement and ascribing to it the nature of an account), would be equally consistent, as in the fiduciary form of an account rendered by the trustee to his principal he invariably charges himself with what he receives and credits himself with what he pays; the most familiar illustration being the customary form of bank pass book, which is a fiduciary account rendered by a bank to its customer.

Since the year 1495, when the first known treatise on double entry book-keeping was given to the world by an Italian teacher, Lucas de Burgo, the science of book-keeping has provided more than a mere chronological register of pecuniary facts, and while it has developed and broadened to an extent that the application of its profounder principles has been legally established as a learned profession, it is somewhat remarkable that a Balance Sheet, the crowning achievement of its possibilities, should receive the cramped construction of a mere cash account, which no more resembles it than does a heap of bricks resemble a temple, or that it should be given the primitive form of a charge and discharge account, when its real purpose is that of a scientific statement of financial condition at a certain date, and that its capacity to display such condition in all its vividness and fulness should be sacrificed to gratify the fads of theorists and perpetuate an absurdity of table A.

It is apparent that the fiduciary account of the Treasurer of a company is the Cash Book, and that book alone contains the receipts and payments constituting the charge and discharge in chronological order, and to that account alone does the final balance of Cash-on-hand convey any significance in such relation, and consequently its appearance on the Balance Sheet, as the last item on the credit side implies a relationship which it in no wise sustains to a Balance Sheet proper.

To the extent that the directors may be regarded as accounting to the stockholders with respect to transactions other than the receipts and payments of moneys, the Books of Account and not the Balance Sheet constitute the account of the receipt and disposition of all values, and the assumption that the statement of assets and liabilities (showing the ultimate status of the estate), is in any wise the subject of, or that the items thereon collectively or severally represent, the composition of a Charge and Discharge Account, or should be arranged with reference to giving expression to any such implication, is too palpable an absurdity to call for further argument.

In the preparation of a Balance Sheet the accounts or items should be grouped and displayed in such manner as to convey the fullest information possible, as follows:

A double sheet of journal-ruled paper containing double money columns on each side is laid open like a book.

Commencing with the most available asset, namely, Cash, the amounts lodged in the several banks, and the amount in hand are separately stated and the figures placed in the indent or first column adjoining the text and the total extended into the next or final column.

The properties actually in the possession of the estate, such as land, buildings, plant, equipment and stock-in-trade, should be stated next, placing the separate values of each in the first column and extending the total of all into the outer column, giving full particulars of deductions for depreciation and basis of valuation to the extent that responsibility therefor is to be assumed.

Bills Receivable being more enforceable or generally more readily realized upon would take precedence over Open Book Accounts in the order of arrangement, and the latter should be classified into good and doubtful, and necessary provision for losses on bad accounts should be shown as well as reserve for customary discounts by deducting from the aggregate sum the amounts respectively charged against the profits to provide for such contingencies.

All actual assets thus available for the satisfaction of the liabilities in the event of liquidation should be first stated and totaled before any quasi or speculative assets, such as claims against the private estates of partners when any question as to their realization may exist (as where the same are unsecured or constitute capital deficits) patent rights, good will, or similar conditional values.

In like manner the liabilities on the other side of the balance sheet should be recited in the order of the priority of their claims or powers of enforcing the same against the estate.

Mortgages against the realty, with reference to the properties stated contra, upon which they are encumbrances, loans secured by collateral pledged therefor, and similar items would rank first against the assets.

Bills Payable or other written pledges would precede unsecured Trade Creditors on open account.

After stating and totaling all the liabilities and obligations to outside creditors it would then be proper to state the various Reserve Accounts and the Capital Accounts.

A Balance Sheet thus framed will show first in classified form the actual assets as opposed and in juxtaposition to the actual liabilities, and the total of each, and thereafter the capital or surplus, or both, as qualified by reserves and opposed to speculative or conditional values.

If the capital precedes the liabilities in the same column the total liabilities exclusive of the capital, is not shown, and if conditional values are stated first among the assets, or alternate with them in the order of arrangement the actual assets are not shown, and the degree in which the capital as stated on the balance sheet may be qualified by reserves or surplus as augmenting features, or by fictitious or uncertain assets as diminishing features cannot be expressed without a rearrangement of the statement.

The ledger folio from which the balance is taken should be prefixed to each account stated on a balance sheet.

The absence of any legislative enactment in the United States, rendering compulsory the preparation of Balance Sheets or Revenue Accounts of corporations in any particular form, gives to the accountant much latitude with respect to the forms he may adopt, and while this acts as a drawback in bringing about a uniform mode of stating accounts of the same nature, there is still open to American accountants the possibility of uniting upon the best forms and establishing them by usage, to the end that they may be legally confirmed before legislative enactment makes inferior forms mandatory.

The Double Account form of balance sheet used in England by Parliamentary Companies, particularly railroads, possesses some features which afford interesting study, and the principle involved and the mode of expression peculiar to it, can be employed with advantage in framing the balance sheets of many corporations in this country.

As will be seen from the following extracts from English authors, treating with this form of Balance Sheet, its destinctive feature is the separation of the fixed assets and liabilities from the floating assets and liabilities, the latter forming the general balance sheet while the former are stated in a separate Capital Account, which is credited with the Capital Receipts, both share capital and loan capital, and is charged with the Capital Expenditure, in acquiring the property for which the Capital Receipts were expressly contributed.

Any excess of the Capital Receipts over the Capital Expenditure would indicate the amount of said receipts not yet applied to their specific purpose or employed as working capital, while any excess of Capital Expenditure over Capital Receipts would indicate the expenditure of revenue in fixed assets in addition to the Capitalization.

The balance, either Dr. or Cr. of the Capital Account is carried to the General Balance Sheet in one amount, and may represent in the abstract either an indebtedness of Capital to Revenue for application of Revenue to Capital Expenditure, or an indebtedness of Revenue to Capital for application of Capital to Revenue Expenditure.

Lawrence R. Dicksee, F.C. A., in his work on "Auditing," published in 1892, by Gee & Co., London, writes on this subject as follows:

"PRINCIPLES IN VALUATION OF ASSETS.

"It being the primary object of most ordinary undertakings to continue to carry on operations, it is but fair that the assets enumerated in a Balance Sheet be valued with that end in view; before this subject is pursued any further, however, it is well to acknowledge two *essentially different features* obtaining to different classes of accounts. Certain Parliamentary Companies, constituted for the purpose of undertaking certain definite public works are, on account of the peculiar circumstances under which they were called into existence, required to render their accounts in a manner radically different from that of all other undertakings; the system they are required to adopt is called the Double

Account System. It being required that all capital raised by these companies shall be expended in the construction of the public works (for the construction of which they were called into existence), care was taken by the Legislature to see that this provision is duly complied with; hence a special form of account in which all monies expended in the construction of the works is separated from the General Balance Sheet. Now, in order that this account (the Capital Expenditure Account) might perpetually show that—and how—the capital authorized to be raised had actually been spent only upon the authorized purposes— except a small margin for working capital or contingencies—it was necessary that the actual amount expended on the works alone be debited to the account, regardless of any fluctuations in value that might afterwards occur. It would, of course, have been easy for the Legislature to have provided that any fluctuations that might occur should be duly allowed for in the General Balance Sheet; but, having regard to the fact that no such fluctuation could in any way practically affect the company, so long as it carried on business, and bearing in mind also the fact that it was contemplated that the company should *permanently* carry on business, it would appear that all consideration of these fluctuations was considered superfluous. With an eye to the future, however, and doubtless also with a view to—so far as possible— insuring the business being permanently carried on, it was provided that the company's works (which were required to be kept perpetually at the amount of their initial cost, regardless of their after value) be continuously kept in a state of efficiency, and that the cost thereof be borne out of Revenue. It will thus be seen that the form of the Double Account system arose from the statutory requirement that all capital raised should be used for the carrying out of the works for the execution of which the company was created; and that the principle that, so long as the works were maintained in a state of efficiency their actual value need not be periodically reconsidered, arose from the circumstance that it was contemplated that the work authorized would be permanently carried on.

"How far—if at all—these considerations need affect one's judgment concerning the valuation of the assets of undertakings not specifically covered by the statutes, it will now be necessary to enquire; but it may be mentioned that, inasmuch as Auditors are not compelled to regard the Legislature as the highest possible authority in the matter of Accounts, they are still free to discuss the principles involved upon their merits, even if a sense of logic compels them to admit an anology between the accounts of Parliamentary Companies and those of other undertakings.

"Taking first the case of private traders, whether *sole*, or firms, it is not difficult to see that, inasmuch as no man can reasonably hope to live forever, the business of such an one is ephemeral as compared with that of a Parliamentary Company. It is true that the business may, and frequently does, live longer than its founder, but to do so, involves a change of proprietorship, and what is this?—*a re-valuation of assets*. It will thus be seen that, although there is no necessity to consider the contingency of liquidation (at what are expressly known as "knock-down" prices) not merely the contingency must be faced, but the eventual certainty of a re-valuation. The basis of such a valuation will be that currently known as 'a going concern,' and it will, perhaps, be worth while to consider the meaning of this phrase. So far as it possesses any definite meaning—for, of necessity, the term is an elastic one—the qualification implies 'at such a value as they would stand in the books if proper depreciation had been provided for'—the term 'depreciation' being taken to represent the amount by which the value of an asset has become reduced by effluxion of time or wear. A fluctuation in value caused by external circumstances will also require to be taken into consideration when property changes hands. It is important to remember that it is not really practicable to so maintain the efficiency of assets that no depreciation shall ever exist, and also that private firms are under no statutory requirement to *retain* the whole of their undertaking in tact; the Double Account principle does not, therefore, apply to the accounts of private traders.

"The accounts of what may be termed 'registered' companies next claim attention. These companies, having a perpetual succession, are perhaps entitled to be considered theoretically permanent (although, in practice, they are generally much shorter lived than private enterprises), and consequently the Double Account principle of stating values might be employed (but for the fact that a registered company is under no obligation to retain possession of any of its assets), if it were found practicable to say definitely what were and what were not, Capital Assets. Such a distinction between items that are all included in one Balance Sheet, however, will be generally conceded to be confusing, and perhaps even misleading, while the fact that no particular assets can claim to be considered more permanent than the rest makes a division of the assets into two Balance Sheets very undesirable, if not impossible. The amount, therefore, at which *all* assets are stated in Balance Sheets, except where a special statutory provision to the contrary obtains, should be regulated by the value of such assets.

"In practice assets may generally be divided into two classes: (1) Those *with* which it carries on business, and (2) those *in* which it carries on business; the former may be named PERMANENT ASSETS, the latter FLOATING ASSETS.

"VALUATION OF SO-CALLED PERMANENT ASSETS. The points to be borne in mind here are that wasting may reduce their value, and that fluctuation may increase or reduce their value. So far as wasting is concerned, inasmuch as it has directly contributed to the profits earned, it is clearly an expense with which profit may be fairly charged. The only question is 'HOW?' which will be considered in full under the head of DEPRECIATION. On the other hand, fluctuation is something altogether apart from profit and loss, being merely the accidental variation (owing to external causes) in the value of certain property owned, but not traded in; to carry the amount of such variation to Profit and Loss Account would be to disturb and obscure the results of actual trading, and so render statistical comparison difficult if not impossible. On no account, therefore, should the results of fluctuations affect the Profit and Loss Account. Whether or not it is desirable that such fluctuations should be revealed by the accounts *at all* will be fully considered under the head of SECRET RESERVES.

"VALUATION OF SO-CALLED FLOATING ASSETS. It being the essential feature of these assets that the whole aim of the undertaking is to convert them into cash at the earliest possible opportunity, the element of immediate realization is an essential factor in their value. The only point to remember is that, while a manufacturing

profit is earned only when the manufacture is completed, a trading profit
is only made when sale is completed. Neither profit must be anticipated.
It may be added, however, by way of qualification that, where a manufacture consists of several distinct processes, and separate accounts are
kept of the manufacturing profit earned under each process, there seems
to be no great objection to each process being considered as a separate
manufacture. With regard to what is a trading profit, a most ingenious
argument was once advanced by the present Attorney-General before the
late Mr. Justice Field (*in re Holden v. Faulkner and others*), in which it
was contended that the most scientifically correct method of valuing a
stock-in-trade was to take it at selling prices, less the average trade
profit; it being suggested that any profit realized in excess of the average
was in reality a profit on buying, not on selling, and any profit realized
less than the average a corresponding loss on buying. The argument
passed muster at the time, appears to be plausible, and indicates a system
that would doubtless prove very convenient in practice; but, unless the
profit on different articles was very uniform, would hardly be a safe one
to adopt."

In the intermediate and final examination of the Institute of Chartered Accountants, held June, 1890, as published in 'The Accountant's
Manual," Vol. II, by Gee & Co., London, question No. 6 and answer
thereto, bear so directly upon the matter before us, that we reproduce
them as follows:

"Q. 6. Some companies, such as railways, strike a balance of
their capital receipts and payments, and bring the net amount into their
Balance Sheets; others enter the total capital received and the total
capital expenditure in their Balance Sheets. Which course do you
recommend, and under what circumstances, if any, is the former
method of stating the accounts desirable?

"A. 6. The first method of stating accounts is only necessary or
desirable in the case of railway and similar companies established for
the purpose of carrying out public works, and regulated by special
statutes, for the actual cost or value of the work of such a company, or
the actual amount of money raised, are not necessarily the same as the
debit and credit sides of the Capital Account. The real value is immaterial, and all that is essential is that the capital raised shall go solely

to the work, and that the work, regardless of its value, shall be maintained.

"The second method indicated, i. e., of entering the total Capital Received and the total Capital Expenditure in the balance sheet should invariably be followed, in the case of a company formed under the Companies' Acts, 1862 to 1887.

"The reason why the first class of companies should, and the second class *should not* adopt what is known as the Double Account system, are very clearly shown in the following extracts from Mr. Ernest Cooper's 'What is Profit of a Company?'

" It is worth while to remember that Capital Account, Reserve Fund, and Profit and Loss and nominal accounts, represent in the case of a Companies' Act Company no real debt of the company, and as I shall contend do not represent specified assets, but are included by means of double entry in the books and in the balance sheet, and indicate the amount of the surplus of assets over liabilities. The Capital Account (including reserves and profits) indicates the amount of that undivided, and in a sense indivisible, portion of the assets which belongs to the proprietors of the company. I say 'in a sense indivisible' because an agreement between the partners for division of assets would not constitute a real separation in fact, as all assets would remain parts of one fund, charged with payments of the creditors, and all collectively (but subject to payment of creditors) the property or capital of the partners.

"Although in a limited sense the operations of Parliamentary Companies involve loss in carrying on the business, as for instance, from bad debts; still Parliamentary companies for public works do not, in their Constitution, speaking broadly, contemplate loss, but only expense of collection as a deduction from the income derived from the work, and they have not in practice a Profit and Loss Account.

"Companies Act Companies have the same power of choosing the manner of dealing with their capital in the course of their operations as a partnership, and it is clear that in the case of those classes of companies which give or receive credit, borrow, lend, or deal in money, or trade in goods, the capital brought in by the shareholders becomes inextricably mixed with the other funds, and incapable of being traced or separated. A glance at the balance sheet of a partnership or company of any of the classes mentioned will show this.

"But to make the matter clear, take the Balance Sheet of the London and Westminster Bank, Limited, of 30th June, 1888. We find its capital, including reserves and undivided profits is:

" Using round figures, say	£ 4,700,000
And that there is owing to customers on deposits, etc., . .	25,300,000
	£30,000,000

The Assets are: Cash, ...	£ 7,000,000
Premises, say	500,000
The Advances, ...	17,000,000
And the Investments, ...	5,500,000
	£30,000,000

"Now assume, although I think incorrectly, the premises to be acquired by outlay of capital, and to be on Capital Account, and of the capital. £4,200,000 remain. How can we say which, or what part of the cash and advances and investments is composed of the money received as capital, and which, or what, part is composed of money received on deposit and current accounts? Thus, if these are inseparable or indistinguishable, as they evidently are in fact, how can they be separated by an account? We can only take the undivided whole and show by an account what the fact is, that capital and deposits and current accounts have contributed in given proportions to the composition of the whole of the assets. But when an asset is lost we cannot distinguish the loss as either the loss of an asset composed of capital or of a deposit. We can only say that as the liability to customers for their deposits is not reduced by the loss, the effect of every loss must be to reduce capital or the property of the proprietors. And if we cannot separate the assets representing capital from those representing deposits, for the same reasons we clearly cannot separate the assets which represent the share capital from the assets representing the Reserve Fund or the Balance of Profit and Loss.

"RAILWAY AND OTHER COMPANIES ESTABLISHED UNDER SPECIAL ACTS.

"A number of capitalists seeking to construct a public work, apply to Parliament for power for two principal objects:

"(1) To construct the work.

"(2) To raise a given fund or capital for the purpose.

"Merely incidental to these objects are the incorporation of a company, the acquisition of land, and the carrying on of the work for the benefit of the proprietors; and it is also incidental to the carrying on of the work that it be maintained in working order out of the revenue derived from it.

"The company incorporated acquires no power beyond the two main ones, and such as arise out of, or are incidental thereto.

"The authority to raise money for the work implies:—

(1) The limitation of the capital to the amount authorized to be raised under the power, and

(2) The limitation of the application of all money raised to the work and equipment thereof, and the retention in the work of all money expended upon it, so that debentures of a parliamentary company acquire the nature and most of the incidence of capital, and only in a limited sense can the debenture-holders be considered as creditors.

"The creation of a corporation for the purposes of the work, implies a limitation of its powers to the construction and carrying on of the work.

"A Parliamentary Company cannot sell or pledge, or even abandon (Abandonment of Railways Acts, 1850 and 1869) any part of its work; and it cannot apply its capital to payment of creditors, debenture or other.

"Parliament accords limited liability to the members of Parliamentary Companies (not expressly, but by refraining from imposing liability), and in these companies the stipulation that capital may not be withdrawn, is in effect imposed as in Companies Act Companies, but in a different form, viz.: by requiring the maintenance of the works.

"But the actual cost or value of the work of a Parliamentary Company, or the actual amount of money raised, are not necessarily the same as the debit and credit sides of the Capital Account. The money value may be either more or less than the total to the credit and debit of the Capital Account of a Parliamentary Company, in proportion as the stock or debentures have been issued, at a premium or at a discount. Real value is immaterial (Abandonment of Railways Act, 1850, Sec. 28). All that is essential is that the whole of the capital raised shall go solely to the work, and that the work, regardless of its value, shall be maintained. When maintenance is provided for, the whole of the net revenue must be applied first to interest on debentures and then to dividend.

"It is natural that Parliament should require that before the proprietors are allowed to divide the revenue of the works, it should be ascertained on behalf of the public which has an interest in the work, that the conditions on which the power (usually in effect a partial monopoly) was granted, have been complied with, and, as a consequence, Parliamentary Companies, with unimportant exceptions, are required to prepare and publish and furnish to the Government, accounts showing what Capital has been raised and that it has been applied to the work, or awaits such application, or, in other words, that the Capital raised has been kept separate and intact. The accounts show whether the contract entered into with the Legislature, if I may so describe it, has been carried out.

"Out of this necessity of keeping the capital funds distinct from the Revenue in Parliamentary Companies, arises necessarily what is known as the 'Double Account System.'

"The keeping of Capital and Revenue as distinct accounts constitutes neither a privilege nor a restriction, but is merely the recording of facts, which Parliament in the public interest requires shall exist in the case of Parliamentary Companies. In Companies' Act Companies the public is not interested any more than in partnerships, and Parliament does not require that any particular state of facts shall exist, nor does such a state of facts usually exist in the circumstances of Companies' Act Companies, and if the fact to support the double account does not exist, the account cannot be prepared."

We have drawn somewhat heavily upon English literature, and treated with the legislative requirements peculiar to England's Parliamentary and Registered Companies, for the reason that the *principles* of accountancy that are involved, if not the *Legislation* that gives them such prominence, are universal the world over, and, in anticipation of the growth of accountancy in the United States and possible future legislation requiring the consideration of the same principles, we deem it better to call attention to them, through the literature of the country where they have become confirmed by law and usage, and so give due credit for their conception and the evident thought and care bestowed upon them, than to present them as mere abstract theories, to the exclusion of their practical and actual application.

We here append three forms of Balance Sheets, namely: (1) Continental Form; (2) English Form for Registered Companies; (3) Double Account Form for Parliamentary Companies.

BALANCE SHEET AS AT 31st DECEMBER, 18.., OF THE .... CO.
(Continental and American form.)

Assets.	$	$	*Liabilities.*	$	$
Cash in Bank . .			Encumbrances on Properties,		
" " Till . .			as under:		
Investments, per Schedule A			Mortgages,description etc:		
Properties, as under:			Bonds .		
Land.per LedgerValuation			Interest due and accrued		
Buildings, "			Sundry Trade Creditors, as		
Leasehold. " "			under:		
Plant. Machinery. etc.			Bills Payable,		
Less Depreciation. .			as per Schedule D,		
Stock in Trade as taken			Open Book a/cs,		
and valued by Mr. ——			as per Schedule E,		
Sundry Trade Debtors, as			Sundry Unpaid Charges, i. e.:		
under:			Taxes, Wages, etc., and		
Bills Receivable,			Special Accounts .		
as per Schedule B,					
Open Book a/cs, Good,					
as per Schedule C,					
less Reserve forDiscounts					
Open Book a/cs, Doubtful					
less Reserve for Bad					
Debts.					
Good Will, or other Speculative Values, more or less likely to constitute mere loading . . .			Capital Account, (or Capital Stock)		
			Reserve Account .		
			Profit and Loss Account .		

DR.   BALANCE SHEET OF THE .... CO., 31st DEC. 18..   CR.
(Registered Co. form.)

Capital and Liabilities.	£ s d	£ s d	*Property and Assets.*	£ s d	£ s d
Capital, showing No. of shares			Property held by the Company, viz:		
Amount paid per share, .			Freehold, Land & Buildings,		
Calls in arrears, Forfeited			Leasehold, " "		
shares, etc., ...			Stock in Trade, ...		
Debts and Liabilities, viz:			Plant at cost, less depreciation, ...		
Mortgages and Debentures,			Debts owing to the Company, viz:		
Debts on Acceptances, .			Secured, ...		
Trade Debts, ...			Unsecured, ...		
Law Expense, owing,			Bad or Doubtful, ...		
Interest on Debentures, "			Debt, if any, due from Director or Officer of Company,		
Unclaimed Dividends, .			Cash and Investments, viz:		
Other Debts, ...			Nature of Investment, and		
Reserve Fund, ...			rate of Interest, . .		
Profit and Loss, ...			Cash, where lodged, and if bearing interest, ...		
Contingent Liabilities, . .					

The incidents of any particular business might call for modifications of the above, which are merely skeletons of the respective forms.

RAILWAY COMPANY.

DR. (Double Account form, Parliamentary Co.)
Receipts and Expenditure on Capital Account.
CR.

	Amount expended to.........	Amount expended half year.	Total.	By Receipts:	Amount received to.........	Amount received half year.	Total.
To Expenditure:							
" On Lines, open for Traffic,				" Shares and Stock, per account,			
" On Lines, in course of construction,				" Loans, " "			
" Working Stock,				" Debenture Stock, " "			
" Subscription to other Railways,				" Sundries (in detail) "			
" Docks, Boats and other special items,							
" Balance, carried to General Balance Sheet,							

GENERAL BALANCE SHEET.

DR. CR.

Liabilities.	£ s d	Assets.	£ s d
To Capital Account, balance at credit thereof,		By Cash at Bankers, Current Account,	
" Net Revenue Account,		" Cash on Deposit at Interest,	
" Unpaid Dividends and Interest,		" Consuls and Government Securities,	
" Guaranteed Dividends and Interest payable,		" Shares of other Companies not charged as Capital Expenditure,	
" Temporary Loans,		" General Stores, Stock of materials in hand,	
" Lloyd's Bond and other Obligations not included in Loan Capital Statement,		" Traffic Account due to the Company,	
" Balance due to Bankers,		" Amounts due by other Companies,	
" Debts due to other Companies,		" " " Clearing House,	
" Amount due to Clearing House,		" " " Post Office,	
" Sundry Outstanding Accounts,		" Sundry Outstanding Accounts,	
" Fire Insurance fund on Station Works and Buildings,		" Suspense Accounts, if any, to be enumerated,	
" Insurance fund on Steamboats,		" Special Items,	
" Special Items,			

Note.—The Capital Account states the items of Debits and Credits on the same sides as they appear on in the Ledger. The General Balance Sheet reverses them and states Ledger debits on the credit side and Ledger credits on the debit side.

STATEMENTS OF AFFAIRS.

STATEMENTS OF AFFAIRS.

A Statement of Affairs, although in some respects resembling both a Balance Sheet and a Statement of Assets and Liabilities, possesses certain features peculiar to itself and fulfills certain purposes that are beyond the scope and capacity of either of the other two forms to accomplish.

Whereas a Balance Sheet and a Statement of Assets and Liabilities have the same end in view, but differ from each other in the respect that a Balance Sheet is prepared from a ledger kept by double entry, and a Statement of Assets and Liabilities from a ledger kept by single-entry or even less systematic records, a Statement of Affairs may be derived from either of the above sources or in the absence of accounts altogether from the testimony and memoranda of the insolvent debtor and the claims as presented and proven by his various creditors.

A Statement of Affairs has to deal almost exclusively with insolvent estates that are about to or have passed into the hands of an assignee or receiver under a voluntary or a compulsory liquidation, and has for its object, as its name implies, the revealing of the condition of the affairs of the estate with respect to the interest of the creditors and the prospective dividend they may receive.

It is therefore not only necessary to show all of the liabilities that may appear upon the debtor's books but also any others that may be presented and established, as well as all contingent liabilities with respect to indorsement on negotiable paper and to what extent they may rank for dividend by reason of being dishonored by the makers.

Preferential claims, for debts due tothe national, state or municipal government, or for wages and salaries to employees, to the extent that the law provides that they shall be paid in full out of the estate before a general distribution, being a direct offset to the assets, are deducted therefrom and appear among the liabilities as a memorandum only of the separate schedule which they constitute.

The general creditors to the extent that they are fully secured by collateral in their custody or partially secured in the same manner form the subjects of schedules separate from creditors wholly unsecured, and form correspondingly separate items on the Statement of Affairs, the unsecured creditors being generally the largest in number and amount and most vitally interested in the Statement of Affairs constitute "Schedule A," and the partly secured, fully secured and contingent creditors follow in respective order.

The partly secured creditors are stated in the full amount, and the estimated value of the securities they hold being deducted therefrom in an indent column, they appear to rank for dividend only in the net or unsecured amount.

The fully secured creditors are also shewn in the full amount of their claims, which being deducted from the estimated value of the securities in their possession (which they are required to account for to the estate) shows the surplus of securities remaining in their hands as an available asset of the estate.

The schedules supporting these items on the Statement of Affairs, are required to be much more replete with information than the schedules supporting the Balance Sheet of a "going concern;" for while the latter usually require little more than the ledger folio, name and balance of each account, in the schedules of creditors accompanying a Statement of Affairs it is necessary that full information of the nature and particulars of each claim, the manner in which the same is secured, the particulars of the security and the balance, the unsecured portion of the claim, or surplus of securities as the case may be, should be stated in separate perpendicular columns preceded by the names and addresses of the respective creditors, which should be arranged in alphabetical order and numbered consecutively as well.

The liabilities of an insolvent estate are usually ascertained both as to character and amount with slight delay, little difficulty and reasonable accuracy. The assets, however, present quite a different problem, and apart from the cash in bank (which is generally but a small item), the surplus of securities in the hands of responsible creditors, book accounts known to be good for their full amount, and investments of a readily convertible or negotiable nature, all other, and in general the greater part of the assets, have to be regarded under two distinct values, (1) the nominal value, and (2) the actual value, which latter is at best but an estimate of what they are likely to produce, based upon the testimony of the debtor and such further confirmation by expert opinion as may be available.

It is necessary to regard the nominal values, for the reason that they are the values to be liquidated, and to the extent that they fail to realize their stated amounts, the shrinkage has to be separately accounted for and represents the difference between the value of the assets on the basis of a "going concern" or as carried by the debtor upon his books, and the value which they produce at "knock-down prices."

In a Statement of Affairs, therefore, both nominal and actual values of assets are displayed. The former serves to preserve the connection between the statement and the financial books, as well as to indicate the probable shrinkages incident to realization; the latter value is that which really counts and is added up on the statement.

The schedules which are required to be filed by an insolvent debtor under the laws of the various states, consist of simple running schedules of assets and liabilities, giving the names and addresses of the creditors and debtors, the amount of the claims owing to or by the same, and an inventory of the stock-in-trade and other properties in the possession of the estate at the time it is turned over to the assignee, receiver or other trustee who may act as liquidator. These schedules are not required to be brought together into a summarized statement capable of displaying the state of affairs at one view, but are so primitive in construction that, from an accountancy standpoint they cannot be regarded as possessing any technical arrangement or fulfilling more than the barest necessities of the case.

Indeed, it seems to have been the object of the courts to depart as little as possible in all matters of accounts from the simplest and most primitive forms and altogether to disregard the progress that has been made in the science of accounts within the last four centuries; it may be that they are apprehensive that the introduction of technical forms recognizing the principle of double entry and the significance of debits and credits would be prejudicial to public policy, by placing matters of accounts beyond the comprehension of the layman. It is, however, generally conceded that accounts requiring skill in their preparation, and displaying technique in their arrangement can nevertheless be readily understood and the essential facts they embody be clearly apparent to a mind entirely incapable of appreciating the method, skill and painstaking regard for detail that were necessary to their preparation.

The Statement of Affairs we have described, is (at least in the United States) a free or non-official form, but has been frequently used to great advantage in displaying the condition of complicated and involved estates, where circumstances existed of such a nature that the official schedules were of little or no value as a guide for the creditors in determining their interest and procedure.

It is, however, the official form adopted by the English Boards of Trade, and English bankruptcy laws have for years required a Statement of Affairs so prepared, to be filed by every insolvent debtor. The Bankruptcy Act, 1883 (46 and 47, Vict. c. 52), which is amended in some details by the Act of 1890 (53 and 54 Vict. c. 71), *inter alia*, also require a Deficiency Account, where possible, to be prepared with every Statement of Affairs.

The rigid exactions of the English bankruptcy laws respecting the statements and accounts which an insolvent debtor is required to produce and file, contrast strongly with the varied and, in most instances, scanty requirements that characterize insolvency proceedings in the United States, and the extraordinary opportunities for dishonest failures that consequently exist here, when compared with the condition of things that obtains in nearly all other countries.

It is true that our Courts show every inclination to set aside assignments and enjoin proceedings where obvious fraud has been proven, but in most of such cases the debtor not being required by law to submit any adequate evidence of his good faith, and having had ample opportunity to conceal or destroy any evidence that might be discovered against him, these proceedings are generally limited to the concern of some one creditor, the extent of whose interest goaded him to the costly, and ofttimes impossible, task of legally proving a fraud which was morally most palpable.

There have been many attempts to institute a uniform Bankruptcy Law throughout the United States, and make due provision for protecting alike the interests of creditors and of the honestly unfortunate debtors. The subject has been agitated from time to time, but only to subside and leave us with nothing better than the conflicting and varied laws of the different States, none of which appear to have duly considered the importance of adequate and systematic *accounting*, and while seeking to establish many excellent points of LAW, seem to have totally disregarded *the only means* for establishing the points of FACT by which alone the law could be enforced, and the rights of all parties protected.

We regret, therefore, that no such papers as a Statement of Affairs, and a Deficiency Account, are in anywise legally identified with the insolvency laws of the United States, although the principles expressed in these forms are known the world over, and accountants in the United States are frequently retained to prepare such statements by the creditors of insolvent estates.

In the absence, therefore, of any form that we can call our own, and recognizing the peculiar succinctness, expressiveness, comprehensiveness, and general excellency of the English form of Statement of Affairs and its accompanying Deficiency Account, we reproduce them here. (see page 116.)

It will be observed that, as in the English form of Balance Sheet, the liabilities are stated on the left-hand side and the assets on the right-hand side, and, although we are disposed to reverse these positions on the Balance Sheet, we are also disposed, for the following reasons, to leave the same arrangement undisturbed upon a Statement of Affairs.

In the preparation of a Balance Sheet the normal condition that obtains is one of solvency (an excess of assets over liabilities), and the

STATEMENT OF AFFAIRS.

Gross Liabilities.	LIABILITIES (As Stated and Estimated by Debtor.)		Expected to Rank.	ASSETS (As Stated and Estimated by Debtor.)		Estimated to Produce.
£ s d		£ s d	£ s d		£ s d	£ s d
99,600.0.0	Unsecured creditors, as per list (A), . . .		99,600.0.0	Cash at Bankers, . .	2,625.0.0	
				in hand, . . .	375.0.0	3,000.0.0
75,000.0.0	Creditors, fully secured, as per list (B), . .	75,000.9.0		Property as per list (G), viz.: . , . . .	*Estimated Cost.*	
	Estimated value of securities, ...	107,500.0.0		(a) Stock-in-trade,	12,500.0.0	7,000.0.0
	Surplus to contra, , .	32,500.0.0		(b) M a c h i n e r y, trade, fixtures, fittings, utensils, etc., . , . .	30,000.0.0	10,000.0.0
13,750.0.0	Creditors, partly secured, as per list (C),	13,750.0.0		(c) Farming stock, growing crops, & tenant rights,	3,750.0.0	2,000.0.0
	Less estimated value of securities, . . .	6,125.0.0	7,625.0.0	(d) Furniture, . .	1,500.0:0	500.0.0
	Other liabilities, as per list (D), ... Of which it is expected will rank			(e) Other property,	1,625.0.0	1,000.0.0
400.0.0	against the estate for dividend, . .		400.0.0		49,375.0.0	
	Liabilities on bills other than debtor's own acceptances, as per list (E), ... Of which it is expected will rank	86,250.0.0		Book debts per list (H), viz.: . . . . Good, . . .		4,125.0.0
16,250.0.0	against the estate for dividend, . .		16,250.0.0	Doubtful, . .	1,500.0.0	
	Preferential creditors, as per list (E), (a) For rates, taxes, wages, etc., .	1,200.0.0		Bad, ...	1,125.0.0	
	(b) For rent, payable under S. 42 of the Act, ...	800.0.0			2,625.0.0	625.0.0
	(c) For S h e r i f f's charges under S 46 of the Act, estimated, . .	350.0.0		Bills of Exchange or other similar securities as per list (J),		5,000.0.0
2,350.0.0	Deducted contra,	2,350.0.0		Surplus from securities in the hands of fully secured creditors (per contra), . .		32,500.0.0
						65,750.0.0
				Deduct preferential creditors (per contra), ...		2,350.0.0
						63,400.0.0
				Deficiency explained in Statement (K), .		60,475.0.0
207,350.0 0			123,875.0.0			123,875.0.0

STATEMENT K, DEFICIENCY ACCOUNT.

To Deficiency, as per Statement of Affairs,	£ 60,475, 0. 0	By Loss on Trading, per Trading Account,	£ 35,250, 0. 0
" Capital, brought into the business at its commencement, and subsequently at various dates,	40,025, 0. 0	" Loss on Shrinkage in value of Assets as estimated and exhibited by Statement of Affairs, viz:	
		Stock-in-Trade, £5.500, 0. 0	
		Machinery, 20,000, 0. 0	
		Farming Stock, 1.750, 0. 0	
		Furniture, 1,000, 0. 0	
		Other Property, 625, 0. 0	
		Bad & Doubtful Debts 2,000, 0. 0	
			30,875, 0. 0
		" Bills Discounted, estimated to rank	16,250, 0. 0
		" Drawings for Private Expenses,	18,125, 0. 0
	100,500, 0. 0		100,500, 0. 0

order in which the mind naturally engages in contemplating its opposing elements is to regard first the assets (or greater amount), and thereafter the liabilities (or lesser amount), so that in departing from the technical form of Balance Sheet and the consideration of sides, and adopting the report form, it is customary to first enumerate the assets and total them, and next and under the assets, to enumerate the liabilities, and deducting the total thereof from the total of the assets above them, to show the Capital or Surplus as the difference or remainder.

However, in the preparation of a Statement of Affairs, the invariable condition that obtains is one of insolvency (an excess of liabilities over assets), and the order in which the mind naturally engages in contemplating its opposing elements is to regard first the liabilities (or greater amount), and thereafter the assets (or lesser amount), so that in departing from the technical form of a Statement of Affairs and the consideration of sides, and adopting the report form, it would be necessary to first state the liabilities and total them, and next and under the liabilities to state the assets, and deducting the total thereof from the total of the liabilities above them, to show the Deficiency as the difference or remainder.

This consideration is even more obvious in a Statement of Affairs than in a Balance Sheet, for, whereas in the latter a greater degree of equality attaches to the certainty of values on either side, in a Statement of Affairs the element of certainty as to value attaches almost exclusively to the liabilities, while the assets are only *expected* to produce the values set against them, and it is but natural that known quantities should be first established before unknown quantities are speculated upon.

As a Statement of Affairs, therefore, is prepared generally in contemplation of its use in insolvency proceedings and, although not an official paper in the United States, is liable to come under official scrutiny, the fact that the law provides that in all official schedules of insolvent estates the liabilities shall be stated first and the assets thereafter, it would seem advisable to disregard any debit and credit significance to the sides of the Statement of Affairs and consider the left-hand side as the First, the summary of the schedules of liabilities, and the right-hand side as the Second, the summary of the schedules of assets, thereby conforming in this particular to the requirements of the courts, and, at the same time, taking advantage of the technical form of statement, to display the liabilities and assets simultaneously on opposite sides and indicate the cross references, contra deductions, and similar features that materially add to the clearness and expressiveness of a statement so prepared.

Another point of contrast between Balance Sheets and Statements of Affairs is, that while a Balance Sheet is a summary of Balances of ledger accounts inseparably identified with the law of debits and credits governing the values of the accounts themselves, a Statement of Affairs is a summary of schedules of obligations and assets which may or may not be recorded in ledger accounts, and are seldom exclusively so recorded. Taking into consideration the numerous qualifying elements to a Statement of Affairs which are entirely extraneous to the books of account and have regard for circumstances as well as for pecuniary transactions, the consideration of the sides of a Statement of Affairs in less technical light with respect to debit and credit than would appear warranted or necessary in the case of a Balance Sheet, and construeing it as a skillfully designed summary of schedules, each possessing its own peculiar characteristics and conveying a distinct purport, would seem to do no violence to any law or principle of accounts.

However, the same argument by which the English accountants justify the sides upon which the assets and liabilities appear upon their form of Balance Sheet is also advanced in support of a similar arrangement upon a Statement of Affairs, and to the extent that the principle involved would appear to be a necessary consideration (in the absence of a construction peculiar to a Statement of Affairs that would justify the reversal of the sides) it would also obtain—but these are considerations which it is unprofitable to lay any stress upon until some form of arrangement of statements of insolvent estates becomes either official, or established by usage in the United States.

A most interesting paper on this subject appears in the June 17, 1893 number of the "Accountant," which treats so ably with the fundamental principles involved that we reproduce it in full, feeling assured that its perusal will prove not only interesting but highly instructive to any accountant whose practice has to deal with insolvent estates in any country.

"CHARTERED ACCOUNTANTS STUDENTS' SOCIETY OF LONDON.

"Statements of Affairs and Deficiency Accounts.

"By Mr. C. R. Trevor, F. C. A.

"A Meeting of this Society was held at the Institute's Hall, on Wednesday, 12th April, 1893, Mr. W. A. Stone, F. C. A., presiding, when the following paper was read by Mr. C. R. Trevor, F. C. A.

"For the choice of the subject on which I am to address you this evening I am indebted to the Committee of your Society, who, having seen the programme of the course of educational Lectures which I have had the honor to deliver at the Owen's College, Manchester, selected this and another subject therefrom, and invited me to address you upon one of them.

"The subject will not, I fear, admit of ornament or enthusiasm, nor is it one of those commanding practical ones which will engage the interest of honorary members in earnest or deliberate discussion.

"In defining a Statement of Affairs, I can most conveniently give you my views of its character by showing in what respects it must be held to differ from a Balance Sheet.

"First, as to what it must contain, and, secondly, as to the sources from which its material must be obtained.

"First—I define a Statement of Affairs to be a complete and carefully arranged document showing : (a) all the liabilities, actual, provisional and contingent, and whether those liabilities are in any way and to what extent secured by the deposit or casual holding of securities of any kind, or by legal equitable mortgage of property or effects of any description; and (b) all the assets according to their nature, condition or localization, set out on fixed principles of valuation, which should be stated therein, and distinguishing those which are free from encumbrance or charge, and consequently available to meet the general liabilities, from those which are subject to charges, which must first be provided for out of their proceeds before there can be any addition therefrom to the general realization; as also those which are in the custody, power or control of other persons than the real owners, and of which there remains only the right of redemption to be counted as an asset.

"Secondly—It will be evident that the investigation necessary to answer these requirements must carry us beyond the ordinary book-keeping; and, whilst the books must be exhaustively used as far as their contents will aid us, we shall soon reach a point where other information will be necessary, and we shall have to consider by what means we can obtain evidence to confirm or otherwise the completeness of the books, and to supplement their records.

"Upon the completeness and accuracy of this evidence will depend the completeness and accuracy of our Statement of Affairs as regards the allocation of creditors unsecured, wholly or partially secured, the free or encumbered assets, and the outlay or expenditure which may be necessary to bring them into a condition for realization.

"The mode in which all these questions must be answered, and the manner of obtaining evidence upon them, can only be taken up in detail in connection with the special character or purpose of the Statement of Affairs.

"This I divide into *"non-official"* and *"official"* or I might otherwise entitle them *"free"* and *"statutory."*

"The *"non.official"* or *"free"* Statement of Affairs is that which is for private and not for public use, in the form of which the accountant is free to use his discretion, so as to set out in the most lucid and intelligible manner the materials he has to deal with in the way of grouping or description, as distinguished from the statutory or official forms prescribed by the Bankruptcy and Companies' Liquidation Acts.

"The former may be chiefly brought into use under the following circumstances: (1) In an investigation for the purpose of ascertaining and reporting on the position of a trader or firm with a view to the satisfaction of an incoming partner; or (2) for the purpose of ascertaining a trader's or firm's position for the satisfaction of bankers or special creditors; or (3) for the purpose of a meeting of creditors of a private character with a view to a settlement by assignment or composition outside of the sphere of the Bankruptcy Court.

"In many, probably in most, of these cases, the form of a Statement of Affairs will be found more suitable than a Balance Sheet, indeed, it may be the only form in which the position of affairs can be suitably set out. For I understand the title "Balance Sheet" to convey that it is founded upon a complete balancing of books kept by double entry, or, at least, kept in such a manner that the results can be safely and readily adapted to double entry form, and Capital and Profit and Loss Accounts deduced therefrom, upon which reliance can be placed without danger to the interests of parties to a contract on either side, when dealing with a business on the basis of a "going concern."

"The three circumstances for which I have suggested the form of a "Statement of Affairs" to be suitable may be taken up together for the general character of the detail:

"*First*, as to the *Liabilities.*—It will devolve on the accountant to satisfy himself that all these are recorded in the books as far as they could show them, or to the date to which the books purport to be written up. If this cannot be fully accepted, or as a supplement to, or confirmation of the books, invoices, statements, Order Books, and Goods Received Books should be examined, at least during the last or current month or quarter, as recent or incomplete transactions might easily be overlooked through their not having reached the stage at which they would come under the cognizance of the book-keeping department. Naturally, the accountant would see that rents, rates, taxes, gas, water, mortgage interests, and any other fixed or periodical charges were brought in from the date of their last maturity as accruing from day to day. If any of these have run into arrears, there may be in the books no clue to their existence, and only careful inquiry, or the casual discovery of papers, may bring them to light. I have known chief rents and ground rents allowed to remain in abeyance for years, the owners considering that, in any event, they were amply secured by the property upon their land, and the tenants looking upon them as claims which could be left out of consideration as long as they were not pressed for payment.

"*Contingent Liabilities* demand careful inquiry and investigation. These may arise in a going concern from:

"(a) Bills discounted, the acceptors of which may have failed, or be of doubtful position, or from endorsement of trade bills which have been passed through without much knowledge of the parties to the bills, or the transactions from which they have arisen.

"(b) Uncompleted contracts which have become unprofitable through fall or rise in values of commodities, and which may have been left in abeyance by one side or the other or both, in the hope of favorable turns in prices, or in building contracts from inability to complete or maintain works for a time, or from imperfections in work only brought to light after possession had been taken.

"(c) Covenants under leases of buildings or of lands to maintain or leave in prescribed condition of repair or annual value.

"(d) Guarantees on suretyships entered into on behalf of others, which could have no record in the books, and would only become claims on failure of discharge by the persons on whose behalf they were given.

"*Disputed Claims* are often the occasions of much difficuly, as the accountant can usually have only one side of the case, and unless he can ascertain conclusively the grounds of contention or resistance of the other side, he can only assess their value according to his best judgment on such evidence as is within his reach. It would, however, be the safe course to discount somewhat the leaning to make light of the opponent's case and to estimate such claims rather in excess of the representations of those on whom they are made.

"The allocation of creditors holding security will, of course, depend upon the mode of valuing such securities—to be spoken of afterwards.

"Next, I refer to the *Assets*. The books should at least show the *debts* owing to the business; but there might, on this side, be deliveries or works uncompleted. Also, the debts should be reduced to net value by deduction of any Trade or Cash Discounts to be allowed on settlement, or Allowances which may be claimed. In some manufacturing businesses these are frequently heavy and uncertain, and some margin in such cases must be provided. Then comes the question, always difficult for an accountant, of classification, as *Good*, *Doubtful*, or *Bad*, in which length of standing would at least lead to enquiry and would supplement any personal or local knowledge of persons. The accountant may here be able to assist his clients by his opportunities for obtaining confidential information or opinions of the standing of debtors. In most cases it would be safe to allow a percentage for loss over and above known weakness, especially where the debts are small or widespread, or long credit is given, or where, in the nature of the business, disputes are likely to arise,

"The value of Stocks should be verified by a practical valuation or inspection, if the circumstances will allow of this being obtained. In the case of an incoming partner there may be practical knowledge by which the accountant should be relieved of responsibility, except as regards the arithmetical accuracy of the figures. In the case of an investigation for a special creditor the accountant should seek authority and permission to obtain a practical opinion upon the general inspection of the Stock Book, but where the circumstances would not permit of this, he must clear himself of a responsibility which lies beyond the scope of his actual knowledge by the most careful enquiries as to cost or current or selling values, and must report the extent to which his responsibility must be limited.

"The value of Plant and Machinery should in all these cases be proved by valuation either made for the occasion or of recent date. The amounts standing in the books (if any) are often little to be relied on. If, however, they represent actual cost, which can be proved, and have been properly reduced by depreciation, they may be sufficiently reliable for the purpose of our first and second occasions. In the case of a statement for a private meeting of creditors, most generally time would not admit of valuations being made for the occasion, but for the purpose of a composition a committee of practical creditors would most likely be appointed to look into and report to a subsequent meeting on the value of assets generally and the sufficiency of an offer.

"In all such cases the fitness of Plant and Machinery for the purposes of the business in the face of new inventions and improvements is an important consideration most difficult to reduce to exact proportions. Hypothecation of Stocks or Goods held in own or other business premises sometimes comes to light under such circumstances. Careful enquiry under this head is necessary to avoid the consequences of concealment which may be resorted to in order to bolster up a favorable position of affairs. The Stock Accounts will often include goods held by other parties for the purposes of the business as goods with bleachers, dyers, or finishers in the textile trade, which, in the case of a suspension, would be retained to cover debts on current account and only released on full discharge of all claims, whether admitted or disputed. Also, goods in transit would be subject to detention to cover claims for carriage of those goods or previously owing.

"The existence of accommodation bills in cases of tightness or the need of assistance sometimes arises. These require close investigation, the more so as those who have entered into such shady transactions usually look on them as only temporary makeshifts which will speedily right themselves, and desire to conceal their character, endeavoring to pass them off as ordinary transactions. Experience proves that they are very frequently the beginning of an end, and they give a very unfavorable aspect to affairs in which any tightness or difficulty has been manifested.

"In the case of a statement of affairs for a private meeting of creditors, it is highly advisable that time should be allowed for getting in from the creditors statements of their claims for verification by the books or from other sources; and, where doubt exists, to ascertain whether claimants are really creditors in fact, or only contingent or disputed. Also it is important that creditors holding any sort of security should be requested to give particulars thereof, and to state the value they put upon it. If they can be induced to give this information the preparer of the statement will be greatly assisted in the classification of creditors as wholly or partially secured, which will have an important effect in bringing out the comparative totals of liabilities and assets. The contingency of a "break-up" must also be considered, and as far as possible an estimate should be formed of the probable depreciation in realization of stocks, plant, and fixed assets in such a result. If possible, an alternative statement showing how liabilities would be increased and assets reduced should be prepared, as not only would reduction in selling value result, but also creditor's securities and their allocation would be affected, and the liabilities might be greatly increased thereby

"Claims for wages, salaries, rents, taxes, and rates must be considered in such a contingency as likely to be increased, and full provision for such increase must be made and their preferential position be recognized according to the terms of "The Preferential Payments Act" by deduction from the value of the assets prior to distribution. Rent payable in advance is often an important item as reducing the available value of assets.

"An accountant called in to prepare such a statement should be careful to hold himself independent of any special interest on behalf of a debtor or any particular class of creditors, and should seek to estimate every item at its fair value in view of its realization, whether as a going concern or in view of a break-up.

"The 'official' or 'statutory' statement of affairs must be in the forms prescribed by the General Rules issued under the Bankruptcy Act of 1890, and dated November 26, 1890, as regards bankruptcies, and by the General Rules made pursuant to section 26 of the Companies' (Winding-up) Act, 1890, and dated November 29, 1890, as regards companies going into liquidation under that Act.

"The first is found at page 28 of the Bankruptcy Rules, and must be verified by a form of oath to be sworn by the bankrupt, in which he avers that the statement and the several lists accompanying it are to the best of his knowledge and belief a full, true, and complete statement of his affairs, the columns and headings of the lists or schedules containing sufficient directions for filling them up, and each list must be separately signed by the bankrupt and dated.

"Under the liabilities the following points require attention:

"First—The date of contraction, and the consideration for each debt must be stated, also as regards securities, the dates when given, and the estimated values and the particulars of bills of exchange and promissory notes held by creditors.

"Second—Under Schedule D, liabilities on bills, there is a column headed 'Accommodation Bills', in which the amount of each must be inserted separately from the column 'Other bills', but no explanation of the terms or nature of the accommodation is here asked for.

"Third—There is a separate schedule for 'Contingent or other liabilities', in which full particulars of all liabilities not otherwise scheduled must be given, with the date and nature of liability. All contingent liabilities, which I have previously referred to, would come in here.

"Fourth—In Schedule G, preferential creditors, provision is made for part of the liability only ranking as preferential, and the rest as ordinary or unsecured. This would provide for the case of salaries or wages owing beyond the limits of the Preferential Payments Act, also for rates and taxes not within the provisions of that Act.

"Under the assets there are many heads which appear separately on the front sheet, and are again enumerated under Schedule II, 'Property', as defined by section 68 of the Bankruptcy Act, 1883.

"Schedule I is to contain debts due to the estate, giving, besides the date of contraction, the folio of ledger or other book where particulars are to be found, and particulars of any securities held for such debts. Both the amounts due to creditors and those due by debtor are to be taken net after deducting any contra claims.

"Schedule I is to contain Bank of England promissory notes, etc., available as assets, with particulars of any property held as security for payment.

"The forms allow no space for insertion of particulars of assets, such as stock, machinery, life policies, &c., nor for showing on what principles, or on what authority their value has been ascertained. It is the debtor's place to fill up this statement, or to have it filled up for him, and the Official Receiver has power to allow a small sum to be paid out of the estate for the services of an accountant in filling it up, if the position of the debtor and the nature of his business justify it.

"Many points contained in this form are suggestive of such explanation as is highly desirable, but not always given, in statements prepared for private meetings, and I would earnestly commend these points to notice in the preparation of the 'non-official' statement which I have already described.

"Life policies require a careful ascertainment of all particulars, such as name of office, date, term (whether whole life or endowment), premium, when and how often payable, also whether during whole life or ceasing at a certain date, the present age of the assured, and the amount of bonuses added. A rough-and-ready mode of valuation has sometimes been adopted by taking one-third of the premiums paid, but this is by no means a safe estimate; as the scale of surrender values given by offices varies, and the duration of the policy greatly affects the ratio of its value to the premiums paid.

"The preferable course is to obtain from the insuring office its own certificate of the surrender value of the policy and bonuses attached to it. If this cannot be obtained, the following mode of a fair average valuation should approximately agree with that of the offices. Ascertain the expectation of life according to the Life Offices Tables, then by the second of Smart's Five Tables contained in *Inwood* or *Jones on Annuities*. The present value of one pound due at the end of so many years, which, multiplied by the number of pounds assured by the policy, will give the present value of the policy, if no future premiums had to be paid. If the policy be for whole life, the expectation will give the number of yearly premiums to be provided for, or if the number be limited, and less than the expectation, the present value of one pound per annum for the number of years will be found by Smart's Fourth Table, and this multiplied by the number of pounds in the yearly premium will give the present value of the premiums, which, deducted from the present value of the policy, will give the net present surrender value.

"There may, of course, be other factors to be taken notice of, which cannot be described here, but which must be carefully brought into account. I am giving these hints from an accountant's point of view, in the absence of assistance from an actuary, which should, of course, be sought in complicated cases.

"The forms of statement of affairs under Companies' Liquidation are contained at pp. 54 and 56 of the Rules. The *first*, as regards creditors, corresponds almost entirely with the form for bankruptcy, the only difference being in the introduction of matter only applicable to companies, viz.: Loans and debenture bonds, which, with *preference* creditors, must be deducted from the assets as the first charge thereon. Also unpaid calls for List K. The *second* is, as regards *contributories*, show-the capital issued and allotted under the several titles of Founders', Ordinary, and Preference Shares, to be set against the estimated surplus (if any) after providing for the claims of creditors.

"Both statements must be attested by an affidavit of some person who is held responsible to give the information by Sect. 7 of the Companies (Winding-up) Act 1890.

"Lists of shareholders of every class must accompany the Statement II. in the forms of Schedules L, M, and N.

Deficiency Accounts.

"The complement of a Statement of Affairs, at least for a meeting of creditors where deficiency may appear, is a Deficiency Account, just as the complement and proof of a Balance Sheet are the Profit and Loss and Capital Accounts, or *vice versa*. This is recognized in the Bankruptcy Act 1883, which requires the trader or debtor to file both accounts. In the Deficiency Account, the trader debits himself with the amount of his deficiency and shows on the credit (right) side of the account, how he and his books account for it, i. e., he takes credit for losses, expenses and expenditure. On the debit (left) side of the account his deficiency will consist not only of the amount by which his liabilities exceed his assets, but he must also include his capital and profits. This account is an excellent book-keeping exercise. The questions which arise in the preparation of it give scope for a thought_ful application of principles. The Statement of Affairs, according to the prescribed form, also according to just and sound principles, necessarily has the liabilities on the left or debit side, because a man must debit himself, or his estate, or his affairs, with the amounts which he owes; and on the right side he takes credit for his assets at their supposed or realizable value. Hence the excess of indebtedness is on the left (debit) side, and comes down as a debt balance on closing the statement, after having put the amount on the credit to equalize the sides. Thus:

Liabilities,	. .	£25,000 0 0	Assets, . .	£10,000 0 0
			Deficiency carried down,	15,000 0 0
				£25,000 0 0

' The Deficiency Account must consequently commence on the debit side with the balance 'brought down', e. g.:

"*Dr.*

"To Deficiency as per Statement of Affairs,	. .	£15,000 0 0
" Capital at the commencement of the trading,		10,000 0 0
" Profits of the first year,	. . . . . .	1,000 0 0
		£26,000 0 0

"Which amount must be accounted for by the particulars to be contained on the opposite (credit) side. If the books have been correctly

kept and completed by double-entry, they would, on closing entries being put in, furnish all the items required to complete that side of the
account.   I will now continue the account by supposing the items which
might probably or possibly come in in such a case as our debit side of
the Deficiency Account has supposed.

"We have £26,000 to account for, as follows:—

"*Cr.*

"By Loss in trading, 2nd year, ...		£ 500 0 0
" do 3rd year, ...		1,500 0 0
" Loss by fire not covered by insurance, . . .		5,000 0 0
" Bad debts, ...		5,000 0 0
" Losses on joint ventures with I., K. & Co., . . .		5,000 0 0
" Stock Exchange losses, ...		1,400 0 0
" Household and personal expenditures (3 years), . .		3.600 0 0
" Preferential liabilities in respect of rent, rate, etc.,		
in advance, ...		250 0 0
" Depreciation in valuing assets for Statement of Affairs:—		
Stock, ...		1,000 0 0
Plant, ...		2,000 0 0
Debts, . . . , .		250 0 0
" Embezzlement of Cashier, . . , ...		500 0 0
Total, ...		£26,000 0 0

"I need not comment on the recklessness and extravagance of such a
case as this Deficiency Account would disclose, unhappily in its parts it
is not without precedent, although, perhaps, not so as a whole.   For
such cases, the Bankruptcy Court provides the proper treatment, and a
public prosecution the proper tribunal.

"The Accountant" of March 4, 1893, refers to a statement by Mr.
Regestrar Linklater, in which he charges accountants employed to
assist a debtor in preparing his accounts with 'putting in figures to
balance the account, which, in many cases, were unreal.'   This is certainly a serious charge, and one which, if proved, would merit severe
condemnation.   We can all readily imagine, if we have not seen for
ourselves, the difficulty in which a debtor finds himself when he has
kept no regular record of his expenditures, and his books are not
sufficient to show whether he has been making profits or losses.   The
only fact before him is the reality of the deficiency, but to the source

and successive stages by which it has been reached he has nothing to guide him. He calls to mind in a general way that he had such and such losses, and has spent money in certain directions, but cannot tell how much. The accountant can only use such information as the debtor gives him, and whilst showing him how much has yet to be accounted for, urge him to call to recollection the times and circumstances which may assist him in fixing the amount. No accountant who has a character to maintain would go beyond this, and it seems unjust to make a sweeping charge against a body of men whose business and habit is to ascertain facts, and to present them in their true light, with acting falsely to their profession. Only absolute proof would justify such a charge against an individual, and even then truth could not condemn all the flock for the wandering of one black sheep.

Let our motto always be, 'Be just and fear not.'"

A vote of thanks was given to the lecturer, and a similar compliment having been paid to the chairman, the meeting terminated.

TRADING AND PROFIT AND LOSS

ACCOUNTS.

TRADING AND PROFIT AND LOSS ACCOUNTS.

The two main purposes, for which accounts are kept, are to periodically ascertain, (a) the profit or loss made or sustained during the period marked and (b) the amount of the surplus or deficiency, or in other words, the extent of solvency or insolvency at its conclusion. These subjects sustain the relationships respectively of *cause* and *effect* and, apart from the introduction of additional capital or the withdrawal of capital and earnings, will exactly correspond, inasmuch as the increase of surplus or decrease of deficit is equivalent to and the result of profit, and the decrease of surplus or increase of deficit is equivalent to and the result of loss during a specified period.

Consequently, the facts and results of each fiscal period, ascertained by means of the books of account, are given expression with respect to both considerations, and form what is known as a "business and financial statement"; the "business statement", entitled Profit and Loss Account, is a resume of the nominal accounts which deal with the general principle of *revenue;* the "financial statement", entitled Balance Sheet, is a compilation of the real accounts treating with the general principle of *capital.*

The "business statement" which is the subject under consideration may assume a simple or an elaborate form according to the number of elements which it contains and the few or many separate accounts that are maintained therefor.

In addition to showing the details that contribute to it, under the headings of separate accounts, not only the judgment and skill exercised in distributing the items among the accounts composing it but also the classification and arrangement of the accounts in the statement itself will materially add to its efficiency and capacity for displaying many important generalities.

While, therefore, the details of account peculiar to the various classes of business, necessitate a separate study in each instance for the purposes of determining their distribution among accounts best calculated to represent essential and convenient elements of revenue, in bringing them together into a periodical statement, the arrangement which they are ultimately to assume and the consequent form of the statement should be also a matter of careful selection, with the view to giving expression to the following facts:

(1) The volume of business done or the proceeds arising from the transactions in each of the several departments that may be comprehended in the business.

(2) The amount of expenditure or outlay in each of the said departments.

(3) The surplus of the proceeds over the expenditure or the excess of the expenditure over the proceeds, as the case may be, of each department, and of the several departments collectively.

(4) The general expenditures not directly appertaining to any particular department nor forming an element of *cost*, but relating to the conduct and management of the business in its entirety and constituting a general offset to or charge against the profits thereof.

(5) The ultimate profit or loss resulting from the business which may be fairly regarded and stated as its *earning power*, before being qualified by the consequences of excessive or insufficient capital for its needs and the consequent income or expenditure occasioned by purely financial transactions, e. g., interest upon borrowed capital, or division of the profits among the proprietors and *inter se* adjustments, including interest on partners' capital, salary allowances to partners, etc.

In the preparation of a *revenue account*, therefore, in order that it may fulfill the foregoing purposes, it is necessary to make a series of *rests* dividing it into sections, each of which being balanced and the balance brought down marks a successive stage in the progression of the subject and the completion of a material generality which it is desirable to distinguish, and beyond fulfilling the primary object of ascertaining the amount of ultimate profit or loss show the causes resulting in such profit or loss so classified with respect to the principles governing their consideration and their successive dependence and development as to afford means of comparing the corresponding items and results of various periods with a view to the ascertainment of how income may be increased and expenditure reduced or, on the other hand, why income has become reduced and why expenditure has increased.

The advance upon purchase price necessary to charge for remunerative return, when realized is known as "gross profit" and the section of the revenue account which shows the amount thereof is called the "Trading Account" and comes first in order, and while it is credited with the total proceeds, the charges thereto include not only the strict purchases but such other trading charges in addition as may, together with the purchases, compose the total cost upon which the trader computes the advance in determining the selling price.

Where but one Trading Account is conducted it may deal exclusively with opening inventory and purchases as *charges*, and sales and closing inventory as *credits*, and all other charges and credits appear in a following section or Profit and Loss Account; but where several Trading Accounts are maintained for different departments respectively, it is customary to charge to each all expenditure that can be specifically applied to each, in order that the profits or losses strictly derivable from each department may be shown.

However, if the charges to a departmental Trading Account include items not composing part of the cost upon which the advance is computed (and although strictly appertaining to the department and essential to carrying it on partake of the nature of expense and therefore not uniformly increased or diminished by the volume of business transacted in that department), it may be expedient to first charge against the proceeds the elements regarded as cost in order that first the "gross profit" (which would vary in proportion to the volume of business, and maintain at all times an approximately uniform percentage to the cost) would be shown by balancing the account and bringing down the balance and, thereafter, in a second section of the same Trading Account the other charges and the approximate "net profit" of the department would be shown carried to Profit and Loss, subject to such further deduction as might represent the undeterminable proportion in which it drew upon the general facilities of the business.

From the foregoing it is evident that the elements composing a Trading Account should be kept in separate accounts in the ledger and that the prevailing custom of keeping a general merchandise account charged indiscriminately with purchases, return sales, wages of manufacturing hands, freights, duties, and similar items, and credited with sales, return purchases, and cancellations of various items previously charged, necessitates a detailed analysis of said account and a re-distribution of the items it contains under various headings, before the exact sums of the aggregate amounts composing the Trading Account can be ascertained and enumerated.

A separate purchase account, or if several departments are maintained a separate purchase account for each, should be opened in the ledger, should be charged with purchases and credited with all returns and allowances thereof, in order that the net amount of the purchases may be shown by the balance of the account and be transferred in the correct amount to the Trading Account. In like manner, a separate sales account, or if several departments are maintained a separate sales account for each, should be opened in the ledger, should be credited with the sales and charged with all returns and allowances thereof, in order that the net amount of the sales may be shown by the balance of the account and be transferred in the correct amount to the Trading Account.

All other accounts which are to be included in the Trading Account should be made the subjects of separate ledger accounts, in order that the balances thereof may be transferred to the Trading Account in proper classification and order. The inventories of stock-in-trade at the commencement and conclusion of the fiscal periods should be charged and credited respectively, to the Trading Account direct.

The Profit and Loss Account may comprehend the entire subject of a "business statement", in which case the Trading Account will form the first section without any distinguishing title, or, if the Trading Account be separately distinguished or comprise several departmental accounts as previously described, the title "Profit and Loss Account" is given to the second and following sections. It is *credited* with the gross profits from the Trading Account or the credit balances from the departmental accounts and such other sources of income in addition thereto, as may arise within the scope and normal transactions of the business, per se; it is *charged* with all those items of expenditure which relate to the general carrying on of the business, and any losses sustained inevitable to the risk peculiar to the business and which may be fairly regarded as a charge thereto.

The *balance* thus arrived at, representing the profit or loss irrespective of extraordinary causes, fluctuations in the amount of capital, or the effect of purely financial transactions, is brought down into the next section and composes the first item therein.

The elements which have been hitherto excluded are herein dealt with; the income from surplus capital invested in securities, the interest on borrowed capital, the profits or losses arising from speculation foreign to the business proper, interest on partners' capital and salary allowances to partners as conditions governing the division of profits between them or, in the case of corporations, redemption fund and general reserve charges, dividends declared and similar items constituting measures of financiering and division or other disposition of surplus.

This division of the Profit and Loss Account into two sections subserves two important uses; (1) it discloses the degree in which the net profits have been affected by commercial causes and how far by purely financiering operations; (2) the convenience such distinction affords in a subsequent review of the accounts for the purpose of ascertaining the earnings strictly ascribable to the business with a view to its conversion into a corporation, and arriving at a basis of capitalization compatible with the profits that reasonably may be expected will arise from the undertaking, without regard to those causes and effects supplementary to the business which will not thereafter apply.

The Profit and Loss Account being a resume of nominal ledger accounts, it is not the proper account to charge or credit with current items during a fiscal period, and the practice (frequently to be met with) of making it a dumping ground, for bad debts, goods lost in transit, discounts and allowances, cannot be too strongly condemned, as all such items as they occur should be charged under proper headings and only brought into the Profit and Loss Account when the books are closed and the nominal accounts assembled in classified form.

The Profit and Loss Account of either a sole trader or firm is generally closed at the conclusion of each fiscal period, and the net profit or loss is carried to capital account or to the several capital accounts in determined proportions, so that the Profit and Loss Account in the ledger is separately stated for each period and no balance is either brought forward from the preceding or carried to the succeeding period.

The Profit and Loss Account of a corporation continues from year to year and the balance brought forward from the previous period and the balance carried forward to the following period show at their respective dates the surplus remaining, (after setting apart reserves), and disposable for dividends or constituting a general surplus remaining after dividend has been charged; or, on the other hand, if capital has become impaired, the said balances, brought forward and carried forward respectively, show the extent of the impairment as increased, diminished or extinguished by the result of the trading during the intervening period.

Instead, however, of commencing the Profit and Loss Account of any period with the balance brought forward from the previous period, each period forms the subject of a distinct account which is first balanced and the balance brought down and the results of that period separately shown, before the balance from the previous account (which until the completion of the succeeding account has been left standing), is brought forward and qualifies the result of the period just ended, accordingly. Any dividend that may be declared or any transfer of surplus to general reserve is then charged against the accumulated balance and the amount remaining is, after the completion of the next succeeding account, transferred in like manner thereto.

Specific reserves for bad debts, discounts, depreciation, etc., which are direct and proper charges against the profits, are included in the account before the profits of the period are determined and shown by bringing down the balance, while the balance brought forward from the preceding account, dividends declared and reserves prompted merely by conservative considerations, together with the final balance carried forward to the following account, form a separate and closing section.

The following forms of Trading and Profit and Loss Accounts (see pages 139-140) will serve to illustrate more clearly the main principles treated with in the foregoing commentaries.

Form 1.

DR.   TRADING ACCT. CLOTHING DEPARTMENT, Year Ending 31 Dec., 1896.   **CR.**

To Inventory, 31 Dec., 1895,	$25,000 00	By Sales (less returns, &c.),	$48,750 00
" Purchases, (less returns, etc.,	40,000 00	" Inventory 31 Dec., 1896,	26,000 00
" Balance, Gross Profit carried down,	9,750 00		
	74,750 00		74,750 00
To Departmental Charges,	500 00	By Balance, Gross Profit brought down,	9,750 00
" Balance carried to Profit and Loss,	9,250 00		
	9,750 00		9,750 00
To Inventory 31 December, 1896.	26,000 00		

DR.   TRADING ACCT. UNDERWEAR DEPARTMENT, Year Ending 31 Dec., 1896.   **CR.**

To Inventory 31 Dec., 1895.	$5,000 00	By sales (less returns, &c.)	$25,800 00
' Purchases (less returns, etc.)	20,000 00	" Inventory 31 Dec., 1896,	3,500 00
" Balance Gross Profit carried down,	4,300 00		
	29,300 00		29,300 00
To Departmental Charges,	300 00	By Balance Gross Profits brought down,	4,300 00
" Balance carried to Profit and Loss,	4,000 00		
	4,300 00		4,300 00
To Inventory 31 December. 1896,	3,500 00		

DR.   TRADING ACCT. HAT DEPARTMENT, Year Ending 31 Dec., 1896.   **CR.**

To Inventory 31 December, 1895,	$7,000 00	By Sales (less returns, &c.),	$16,200 00
" Purchases (less returns, etc.),	8,000 00	" Inventory 31 Dec., 1896,	1,400 00
" Balance, Gross Profit, carried down,	2,600 00		
	17,600 00		17,600 00
To Departmental Charges,	200 00	By Balance, Gross Profit, brought down,	2,600 00
" Balance carried to Profit and Loss,	2,400 00		
	2,600 00		2,600 00
To Inventory 31 December, 1896,	1,400 00		

DR.   PROFIT AND LOSS ACCT.—A, B & C—For the year ending 31 Dec., 1896.   **CR.**

To Rent,	$2,000 00	By Profit Clothing Department,	$9,250 00
" Salaries,	4,100 00	" " Underwear do	4,000 00
" General Expense,	1,400 00	" " Hat do	2,400 00
" Cartage,	800 00	" Discounts on purchases,	1,450 00
" Depreciation,	300 00		
	8,600 00		
" Balance Carried down,	8,500 00		
	17,100 00		17,100 00
To Interest on Loan, 100.00		By Balance brought down,	8,500 00
" " " Capital, 400.00	500 0		
" Balance, being Net Profit, Divisible as under, viz:			
A ½ 4,000,			
B ¼ 2,000,			
C ¼ 2,000,	8,000 00		
	8,500 00		8,500 00

Form 2.

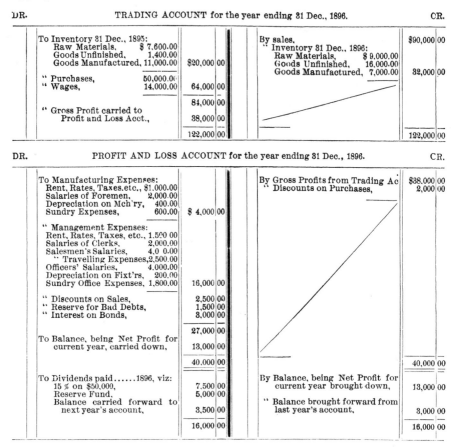

DR.   TRADING ACCOUNT for the year ending 31 Dec., 1896.   CR.

To Inventory 31 Dec., 1895:			
Raw Materials, $ 7,600.00			
Goods Unfinished, 1,400.00			
Goods Manufactured, 11,000.00	$20,000 00		
" Purchases, 50,000.00			
" Wages, 14,000.00	64,000 00		
	84,000 00		
" Gross Profit carried to			
Profit and Loss Acct.,	38,000 00		
	122,000 00		

By sales,	$90,000 00
" Inventory 31 Dec., 1896:	
Raw Materials, $ 9,000.00	
Goods Unfinished, 16,000.00	
Goods Manufactured, 7,000.00	32,000 00
	122,000 00

DR.   PROFIT AND LOSS ACCOUNT for the year ending 31 Dec., 1896.   CR.

To Manufacturing Expenses:		
Rent, Rates, Taxes.etc., $1,000.00		
Salaries of Foremen, 2,000.00		
Depreciation on Mch'ry, 400.00		
Sundry Expenses, 600.00	$ 4,000 00	
" Management Expenses:		
Rent, Rates, Taxes, etc., 1,500 00		
Salaries of Clerks, 2,000.00		
Salesmen's Salaries, 4,0 0.00		
" Travelling Expenses,2,500.00		
Officers' Salaries, 4,000.00		
Depreciation on Fixt'rs, 200.00		
Sundry Office Expenses, 1,800.00	16,000 00	
" Discounts on Sales,	2,500 00	
" Reserve for Bad Debts,	1,500 00	
" Interest on Bonds,	3,000 00	
	27,000 00	
To Balance, being Net Profit for		
current year, carried down,	13,000 00	
	40,000 00	
To Dividends paid......1896, viz:		
15 % on $50,000,	7,500 00	
Reserve Fund,	5,000 00	
Balance carried forward to		
next year's account,	3,500 00	
	16,000 00	

By Gross Profits from Trading Ac	$38,000 00
" Discounts on Purchases,	2,000 00
	40,000 00
By Balance, being Net Profit for	
current year brought down,	13,000 00
" Balance brought forward from	
last year's account,	3,000 00
	16,000 00

The first form has three departmental acccounts showing the gross profits of each qualified by charges appertaining thereto, and the final balance of each is carried to the Profit and Loss Account, in which account appear the general management expenses.

The balance of the Profit and Loss Account at that point is then brought down into the following section, where also appear the charges for interest on loans, interest on capital, and the division of the net profit among the partners.

The second form relates to the business of a corporation engaged in manufacturing. The Trading Account deals strictly with cost as against proceeds and the gross profit therefrom is carried to Profit and Loss

Account, which account is charged with manufacturing expenses, general management expenses, discounts, reserves, and interest on bonds, the balance representing net profit is brought down to the credit of the following section supplemented by the balance from the previous year and the total is disposed of by dividend, amount carried to reserve, and Balance carried to the next year's account.

These pro forma accounts, which have been filled out with figures to more clearly illustrate their workings, are necessarily but bare outlines of the forms they would actually assume, as the conditions of any particular business would inevitably introduce special features and call for elaboration of detail.

Furthermore, the forms presented bear a closer resemblance to the ledger accounts than to prepared statements, as in the latter case the inventory at the conclusion of the period would be deducted from the opening inventory and purchases, leaving the sales alone as the *proceeds*, opposed to the value of goods disposed of as the *cost*.

In *"The Accountant"* of November 11, 1893, is published a lecture delivered before The Chartered Accountants Students' Society of London by Mr. Lawrence R. Dicksee, F. C. A., on the subject of ''Forms of Accounts and Balance Sheets.''

In the course of his lecture Mr. Dicksee discusses Trading and Profit and Loss Accounts, and his remarks being apropros, we take the liberty of quoting the following extracts.

*   *   *   *   *   *   *   *   *   *

''It will thus be seen that the efficiency of this account depends very materially upon the skill with which the income and expenditure have been distributed over the various headings employed; and consequently, if we are to profitably consider the question, it becomes necessary for us to discuss the nature of the various headings under which the items of this account should be divided.

''It follows that, inasmuch as this account details for our consideration the summarized result of the transactions recorded in the books, the nature of the account itself will very materially depend upon the precise business which is being carried on, and it therefore becomes necessary for us to further consider the subject under the heading of various classes of business.

"Taking first commercial concerns (which undoubtedly represent the great majority of the undertakings which we are now considering) we find that the transactions consist in the buying of goods and the selling thereof, either in the precise form in which they were purchased (as in the case of traders), or in an altered form (as in the case of manufacturers); in both cases there being the further expenditure incidental to the carrying on of the undertaking.

"Dealing first with the Accounts of Traders, which are naturally of a simpler nature than those which require to be kept by manufacturers, the first circumstance which strikes us is the method usually in vogue by which a trader computes the amount of advance upon purchase price which it is necessary for him to charge for his goods in order to obtain a remunerative return for his labor, and this excess is very generally known by the term of 'Gross Profit.'

"It would be very difficult to find an exact definition of the term Gross Profit,' inasmuch as the items from which it is calculated will be found to vary in different undertakings; but seeing that the whole business of a trader is based upon the calculation of a fixed percentage of gross profit upon each different class of goods dealt with, I think it necessarily follows that any form of accounts which does not recognize the existence of such a thing as 'Gross Profit' fails to afford the trader that assistance which he is entitled to look for from his accounts, and consequently to a very great extent fails to justify its existence.

"I have heard it argued by many experienced Accountants that Gross Profit cannot be considered to arise until such things as rent of warehouse, salaries of warehousemen, etc., have been debited to the Trading Account; but as it is the almost universal custom of traders to reckon their percentage of Gross Profit entirely from the cost price of their goods (although as a matter of convenience they actually make the calculation backwards from the selling price) it seems to me that, however correct it may be in theory, it is in practice nothing more than pedantic to include in this first section of the Profit and Loss Account anything more than Sales and the Closing Stock upon the credit side, and Purchases and the Opening Stock upon the debit. It is, of course, quite possible to argue that the resultant credit balance means absolutely nothing at all; but, even if this is so, the fact remains that

unless we so prepare an account it is impossible for us to see, or for the
trader himself to see, whether the aggregate transactions of a period
actually result in the percentage of gross profit which he had been cal-
culating upon throughout the period; and therefore I think that,
whether we choose to call the balance of this first section 'Gross Profit,'
or whether we merely employ the indefinite term 'Balance,' the over-
whelming weight of advantage lies in our bringing our account, in this
respect at least, into accord with the custom of every trader, and so
enabling him to ascertain whether during any period he has actually
achieved the results which he anticipated.

"In the next section of the 'Profit and Loss Account' I would include all those items of income and expenditure relating to the business
except such as may be said to be of a financial nature, such as discount, interest and income-tax, which latter I would relegate at the
third and last section of this account, which also shows the disposal of
the profit among the proprietors or shareholders as the case may be.
Interest upon borrowed capital or upon partners' capital I would also
include under this last section, and also directors' fees; but the salary of
a managing director or of a working partner I should consider more
properly belonged to the second section, which bears the bulk of the
general expenses.

"And here perhaps I may be allowed to diverge for a moment with
a view to consider the justification of debiting the Profit and Loss
Account of a business with either interest on partners' capital or salaries of working partners. It is, I think, unusual to find both these
items charged in the same set of accounts, and that for the simple
reason that in such a case it would be difficult to say clearly what the
remaining balance of profit expressed; it is open to us either to adopt
the view that a partner is entitled to a fixed interest on the amount of
his capital, and that the remaining balance of profit represents his remuneration for carrying on that business; or, on the other hand, we may
assess the value of a partner's supervision at what we think to be a fair
salary, and describe any remaining excess of income over expenditure
as the remuneration belonging to the partner as a capitalist; but if in
our accounts we provide the proprietors with what we consider to be a
fair interest for the use of their capital and also a fair remuneration for

their services as workers, it would appear that there ought, as a matter of fact, to remain no further surplus unless, indeed, it were in the nature of a reserve to be devoted to a fund for the purpose of equalising the results of trading.

"This, however, is a question of theoretical interest perhaps, rather than of practical importance; and we will therefore return to the consideration of the relative advantages of debiting partners' salaries, and debiting interest on capital. I think, perhaps, from a practical point of view, there is less real difference between the two methods than would at first sight appear, for it is obvious that the ultimate results in each case must necessarily be the same; but where partners devote different amounts of time to the business, or where they risk different amounts of capital, the question certainly assumes some importance. Upon the whole, I think that where partners devote equal capital but different amounts of time, it is simpler to disregard interest upon capital, and to charge partners' salaries; but in the case of partners devoting unequal amounts of capital and equal time, that interest upon capital should be charged, rather than salaries. Under both these circumstances, however, the assumption is that the ultimate net profits are divided equally; but where this is not the arrangement of the partners, of course it is more than likely that the inequality of their respective contributions will have been duly taken into consideration when arranging their respective shares.

"Be this as it may, however, the fact remains that such questions of the adjustment of profits between partners *inter se* do not actually arise out of our present consideration (which is solely that of the form in which accounts should be drafted), and it is, therefore, perhaps, hardly necessary that I should discuss the matter further than to suggest what I consider to be the best form of treatment in each case.

"Returning now to our typical Profit and Loss Account of Traders, I may remark that the utility of a division between the second and third sections comes in this way—that if the amount of business and the rate of expenditure have been fairly constant, the balance shown at the foot of the second section will also be constant, irrespective altogether of any fluctuation in the amount of capital which the firm may have had at its disposal; and this I consider extremely useful, both for the purpose of seeing how far the net profits of a concern have been affected by purely financial reasons, and how far by commercial reasons, and also on account of convenience it affords if it should at any future time be decided to convert the venture into a limited liability company."

*　*　*　*　*　*　*　*　.　*　*

"Passing on to the accounts of manufacturers, I think it is first necessary for us to subdivide this heading in accordance with the various classes of business that fall hereunder.　Under the first class is the manufacturer who is but slightly removed from the trader; that is to say, the manufacturer who does not require to sink a large proportion of his capital in expensive plant and machinery—the most typical examples of which are, perhaps, that of the small manufacturing jeweler and the small manufacturing tailor, both of whom, by the way, are fast dying out.　In this class, as with traders pure and simple, we find the selling price based upon a percentage of so-called Gross Profit, the outlay in this case being the cost of materials together with the wages spent in manufacturing; and, therefore, although the method is clearly indefinable from a theoretical point of view, I here again advocate the division between the first and second sections being drawn exactly where it is drawn by the manufacturer himself in his mental calculations. Those who wish to have their accounts as complete as possible may prefer, in addition, to make a further subdivision of this account in the second section, separating the expenses of manufacturing (such as rent of factory, wages paid for supervision of workers, depreciation of plant, etc.) from those expenses which relate more particularly to the storing of goods and the selling thereof; but inasmuch as the balance shown by this break would correspond with nothing in the mind of the manufacturer it appears to me to be superfluous, and personally I prefer to merely show separate totals for these classes of expenditure in the same section."

*　*　*　*　*　*　*　*　*　*

"The manufacturers belonging to the next class are those whose transactions consist in the manufacture of one or more classes of goods involving expensive plant, which goods are first manufactured and then warehoused before being sold. •These undertakings are naturally upon a much larger scale than those which I have just considered, and we consequently find that the accounts are, as a rule, more specifically kept and the method of costing more complete.

"The first section of the account thus becomes divided into two parts, upon what I may call parallel lines, viz:

"The Manufacturing Account, which deals with the conversion of raw material into manufactured articles, and shows us the profit upon manufacture, and the stock of new materials on hand, and

"The Trading Account proper, drawn upon the same lines as first section of a trader's Profit and Loss Account.

"The second and third sections of the account do not show us any new features that call for our consideration."

*   *   *   *   *   *   *   *   *   *

"The next class of manufacturers with which we have to deal consists of those whom I may conveniently summarize under the head of Contractors, i. e., those manufacturers who only make articles which have already been sold (if I may use the term) for an agreed price. To this class belong builders and many engineers.

"It is perhaps more in this class than anywhere else that the absolute necessity of proper Cost Accounts is so evident: I would therefore regard all Contractors' Accounts as incomplete which did not provide, in addition to an ordinary Profit and Loss Account, a Summary of Cost Account showing the same result. This being done, the chief interest centres around the Cost Account rather than the Profit and Loss Account itself, and I therefore think that there is less necessity for the latter to be unduly elaborate. I usually prefer to state this latter account in two sections only, the first section corresponding to sections one and two in the classes of accounts that we have already considered, and the second dealing only with the financial items."

*   *   *   *   *   *   *   *   *   *

"Another very important class of accounts, which can hardly be said to come under any of the previous headings, are those relating to mines. These accounts I think are best dealt with in a manner somewhat similar to that indicated in the case of contractors; that is to say, in one section I would include all the items relating to the actual working of the undertaking, and in the second section those appertaining more particularly to finance: Cost Accounts would be made weekly or monthy, but they would usually form no part of the annual accounts.

"With regard to non-commercial accounts, I think the system of dividing the account into two sections only conveniently applies.

"I may add that the introduction of a separate section for the financial items possesses this further advantage that, in those cases where it is deemed inadvisable to publish full accounts, the published account may conveniently consist of the last section of the Profit and Loss Account only; of course this consideration will only apply in the case of the accounts issued by a company to its shareholders, and in such cases I think when only the final section of the Profit and Loss Account is published it should contain not only the Directors' Fees, Interest on Debentures, Contributions towards Reserve Fund, etc., but also the amount set aside for Depreciation of Plant, Investments, etc.

"This is perhaps the proper place to offer a protest against the method adopted by many companies of stating in their published accounts a so-called 'Net Profit', out of which it is proposed to set aside a certain sum for Depreciation and Directors' Fees. Of course if the Articles of Association provide that the accounts shall be so stated, there is, for the moment no other course to be adopted; but for my own part I would suggest that an opportunity could not be taken too early of altering Articles which produced so clearly misleading a result."

ACCOUNTANCY AND THE LEGAL

PROFESSION.

ACCOUNTANCY AND THE LEGAL PROFESSION.

The employment of Professional Accountants to examine books of account and documents relating thereto, to report the facts disclosed by their investigation and testify before referees and courts in actions at law, both civil and criminal, has become an important part of accountancy practice.

The Accountant is thereby brought into repeated and intimate touch with the Lawyer, and the steady rise in the plane of intellectuality and consequent value of service that has marked the growth of accountancy has done a great deal towards removing the indifferent esteem in which lawyers were once prone to regard accountants.

Whereas accountants of ability and integrity have at all times succeeded in making felt the value of their services and ingratiating themselves in the esteem of such of the legal profession as they have co-operated with, the large number of incompetent persons who have arrogated to themselves the title of "expert" or "professional" accountant, and the fees they have extorted for worthless services, has been, no doubt, the cause of the unfavorable regard entertained for accountants by the legal profession in the past, and their failure to avail themselves of the accountant's services in instances where the same would have been of incalculable advantage.

As ample measures have been taken by the Legislature of the State of New York to insure the fitness of all persons practicing as Public

Accountants (chap. 312, laws of 1896), and as California, Massachusetts and Pennsylvania are likely soon to pass similar laws, the evils above referred to may shortly be expected to disappear, and as the interests of Accountancy and The Legal Profession are in a high degree reciprocal and, if properly understood, capable of being regarded to mutual advantage, it will be the fault of the Accountant if in the future he is not on the best of terms with the Lawyer.

As there is a prejudice to be overcome, however, it is more than ordinarily incumbent upon the accountant when retained upon matters in suit, to exercise the keenest judgment in grasping the situation with respect to his function and the utmost dispatch in ascertaining the facts that are material in the premises—it, of course, being understood that it is the accountant's duty to impartially report upon the facts. The instances that have come to our notice of accountants appearing on opposite sides of a case and reporting different facts, cannot but be deplored as degrading to the profession on the part of one or the other of them.

The responsibility that an accountant assumes in this branch of business is of a grave nature, as upon his report and testimony the case often largely depends.

While the accuracy of his results must, of course, be susceptible of demonstration, he should bear in mind that such demonstration rests upon a *science* with which all are not familiar, and that evidence of his professional integrity (which ofttimes is more relied upon by a judge and jury), must be borne out by courteous and straightforward deportment and testimony when on the witness stand.

He should strive to strip his presentation of the facts of all bewildering technicality and cultivate a power of elucidation which will be at once clear, concise, and consequently intelligible to his audience.

As we believe it will be of interest to our readers to see and judge for themselves of the importance and intricacy of the accountants' report in suits at law, we have appended two specimen reports occurring in actual practice, and while the names of the parties are suppressed and their relationships (in italics) substituted therefor, it will require but slight observation to perceive that neither of these reports is a creation of the imagination.

The first, entitled "A Successful Failure" is a case in which an insolvent debtor, who had gone into business with a capital of a few thousand dollars, after living for several years in relatively sumtuous style, failed for about $100,000; he thereupon informed his creditors that it was unnecessary for him to make an assignment as there was nothing to assign, and that they were welcome to anything they could find.

After the accountants, who were retained at the instance of counsel for the largest creditor, had rendered their report, an offer was made by the debtor to settle at 35 cents on the dollar; the offer was refused and the debtor thereafter indicted by the Grand Jury.

The second, entitled 'Hereditary Insolvency' is a case in which when the father failed the property was found to belong to the son, and when the son failed (after his father's embarrassments had been adjusted), the property was found to belong to the father. This report contains many other interesting features peculiar to itself, and will prove interesting and instructive reading to a student of business finance.

Upon the accountant's report in this case also, the smooth and well-planned course of the debtors received an abrupt check.

A SUCCESSFUL FAILURE.

NEW YORK,...................18..

CITY COURT, NEW YORK.

Contesting Creditor and ano.

vs. } Accountants' Report.

Insolvent Debtor.

Messrs. *Attorneys for Creditors,*

No. .. Broadway, New York.

Dear Sirs:

We beg to submit the results of our investigation of the books of *Mr.* ...., an insolvent debtor and defendant in the above entitled action, for the period of 5 months and 4 days, commencing 15th JANUARY and ending 18th JUNE, 18..

The books and papers submitted to us were as follows:

BOOKS—Sales Book   12th Sept. 18.. to 25th May 18..

       "   "   25th May 18.. to 7th Nov. 18..

       "   "   7th Nov. 18.. to —th June 18.. inclusive.

Cash Book   12th Oct. 18.. to   "   "

Bills Receivable Book   10th May 18.. to   "   "

               with envelope containing description of four notes discounted.

Cheque Book,   )   13th Apr. 18.. to 14th June 18.. together

National Bank of Deposit }   with cancelled cheques Nos. 2419/2558.

Pass Book, Nat'l B'k of Deposit 6th Jan. 18.. to —th June 18.. inclusive.

Collection Book   1st Nov. 18.. to 20th May 18..   "

Stock Journal, without date, containing memo. of Stock to traveling

       Salesmen, etc.

Memorandum Book   2d May 18.. to 13th June 18..

Private Ledger   18th Nov.18.. to 17th June 18..

Creditors'   "   12th Aug.18.. to   "

Debtors'   "   —th Aug.18.. to   "

PAPERS—Letter from *Brother of I. D.*, dated Manchester, 12th Oct. 18..

       Part of Letter from *Brother-in-Law, b. of I. D.*, dated Paris, 11th Aug. 18..

       Three memorandum Cash Balance proof slips, dated 6, 11, 14th June 18..

       Order on *Insolvent Debtor*, signed *Brother*, dated 8th July 18.. favor of

           Confidential Salesman for $20.00.

       Letter signed *Brother*, no date.

       Memorandum of "Bills Payable," as at 18th June 18..

       Statement on printed form of *Bankers*, No. -- Rue St. Georges, Paris,

           dated 26th Sept. 18.., showing money paid by *Brother* in Paris for *a/c* of

           Insolvent Debtor.

       Statement of Losses and Bad Accounts at 15th Jan., years 18.., 18.., 18.., 18..

         "   " Sales   "   "   "   "   "   "   "

       Inventory of Stock and Statement of Book Accounts, Bills Receivable,

         and Book Accounts Payable, as at 15th Jan. 18.., and 15th Jan. 18..

The books of original entry covering the period prior to those submitted to us are missing and we note from the examination of the debtor and other information received by us that the janitor at the debtor's place of business sold them for old paper, together with such documentary records that may have been left with him, and in consequence the only consecutive record of his business remaining in any degree of completeness is embraced in the period covered by this report.

It was at first our intention to endeavor to extract from the Ledger a general summary of prior transactions, and by comparison and analysis to re-discover lost data, but as this process would involve greater time and expense than the immediate purpose seemed to warrant, it was determined after an interview with your client to confine ourselves to the period now under review.

In the statement submitted by the debtor, as of 15th JANUARY 18.., it appears that—

His total Liabilities were	$120,699.32	
" " Assets "	39,128.16	
" " Deficit was		$81,571.16

We correct this statement as follows, and as is fully shown in Deficiency Account on page 9 of this.

ADDITIONAL CHARGES.

Liability omitted by debtor, *A Creditor's Acct.*,	1.00	
Bad Accounts accounted good in Debtor's statement but immediately thereafter written off and obviously known to be bad at the time,	787.90	788.90
		82,360.06

ADDITIONAL CREDITS.

Book Accounts abandoned as worthless but subsequently realized in part to the amount of	422.29	
Arbitrary deduction of 10% on $17,299.12 Book Accounts, etc., part of which was realized subsequently and the actual discounts and losses provided for in this accounting, the remaining part having been assigned to *Mother-in-Law of I. D.* and *Confidential Salesman*,	1,729.92	2,152.21

NET DEFICIENCY.

As corrected and shown in Deficiency Account on page 9 of this,			80,207.85
Apportioned and based upon the debtor's own statement, to wit:			
Losses to 15th Jan. 18..		47,819.85	
" " 15th JAN. 18..	33,751.31		
Net amount of our changes as above stated, i. e., $2,152.21 less $788.90 =	1,363.31	32,388.00	80,207.85

TRADING 15TH JANUARY TO 18TH JUNE 18

A review of the debtor's trading for the five months immediately preceding his failure, shows the following general results, as more fully set forth on page 10 of this.

Net Cost of Mdse, including Factory labor, but exclusive of all other expenses,	$34,623.78	
Total Net Proceeds after deducting Discounts, Returns, etc.,	33,892.71	
Loss, occasioned solely by excess of buying over selling price,		$731.07

PROFIT AND LOSS ACCT., 15TH JANUARY TO 18TH . JUNE 18..

A review of the debtor's management and other expenses, losses, etc., for the five months immediately preceding his failure, as more fully set forth on page 11 of this, and also his personal drawings as therein stated, shows the following additional items:

Factory Rent, Salesmen's Salaries, Commissions and Traveling Expenses,	3,286.50	
Management Expenses, Interest on Loans and Notes, Cash Shortages, Bad Debts, etc.,	2,751,69	
	6,038.19	
Deduct Miscellaneous Credits,	65.95	5,972.24
Total Business Losses, as per Profit and Loss Acct.,		6,703.31
Personal Drawings of *Insolvent Debtor* for private purposes, as per Account shown on pages 23/25 of this,		6,937.95
Add Deficiency (corrected) as shown on page 2 of this,		80,207.85
Total Deficiency at 18th JUNE 18..		93,849.11
apportioned Loss to 15th Jan., 1st yr.,	47,819.85	
" " 15th " 2d "	32,388.00	
" " 18th JUNE 18.., 5 mos.,	13,641.26	93,849.11

STATEMENT OF AFFAIRS AS AT 18TH JUNE 18.., immediately prior to the transfer of Assets.

The debtor's condition upon his failure, disregarding preferences, was substantially as follows:

LIABILITIES.

Due Sundry General Creditors, per Schedule on page 19,		$29,106.17	
" " " " Bills Payable, " " 20,		56,392.68	
" *Mother-in-law* (not including interest) Acct., " 27,		10,600.00	
" *Brother-in-law, b.* (including interest) " " 27,		11,465.62	
" *Brother* " " " " 26,		25,494.74	
" *Wife* " " " " 27,		2,555.59	
" *Confidential Salesman* (" 5 mos. salary) " " 28,		1,966.40	$137,581.20

ASSETS—Book Value.

National Bank of Deposit, per acct. on page 17, $ 16.07 ⎞		
Bills Receivable held as margin, 646.42 ⎠	662.49	
Cash, subsequently paid to *Bro.-in-law b.* per *a/c* page 27,	7,565.60	
Bills Receivable, " handed to " ·" " 27,	1,500.00	
" " assigned to *Mother-in-law and Confidential*		
Salesman, on page 28,	728.09	
Book Accts. Receivable, per Schedule, " 15,	3,461.71	
Brother-in-law, a. amt. paid 12th Apr. 18.., no explanation 26,	114.20	
Merchandise, handed over *a/c Brother*, 26,	28,000.00	
Furniture and Fixtures stated to have cost $2,500 sold out		
by Sheriff under confession of judgment to *Mother-in-law*,	1,000.00	
Mortgage on *Greater N.Y. lots*, assigned to *Mother-in-law* in		
Dec. 18.. as of $1,000 value (see page 7, examination of		
debtor, 25th July 18..),	700.00	43,732.09

DEFICIENCY as hereinbefore stated, 93,849.11

STATEMENT OF AFFAIRS AS AT 18TH JUNE 18.., subsequent to the transfer of Assets.

The debtor's present condition as deduced from the books, etc., submitted to us and corroborated by his testimony upon his examination, after making preference to sundry *relatives*, etc., for alleged amounts due them is substantially as follows:

LIABILITIES.

Due Sundry General Creditors, on open Acct.,		$29,106.17	
" " " " on Bills Payable,		56,392.68	$85,498.85
" *Mother-in-law*,		11,000.00	
Deduct Cash (unexplained),	$ 400.00		
" Mtg. Greater N. Y. Lots,	1,000.00		
" Book Accts. Assigned,	1,200.00		
" Furniture and Fixtures,	1,000.00	3,600.00	7,400.00
" *Brother-in-law, b.* (including interest),		11,465.62	
Deduct Cash,	7,565.60		
" Customers' Notes,	1,500.00	9,065.60	2,400.02
" *Wife*,			2,555.59
			97,854.46

ASSETS—Book Value.

Confidential Salesman, Bills Receivable,	728.09		
part of $3,461.71 Book Accts.,	2,261.71		
	2,989.80		
Deduct Amount due him,	1,966.40	1,023.40	
Brother, Estimated Value of Mdse, handed him			
by debtor,	28,000.00		
Deduct, Amount due him (interest included)	25,494.74	2,505.26	
Brother-in-law, a. Amount paid 12th April 18..,			
unexplained,		114.20	
National Bank of Deposit, Balance per Pass Book,	16.07		
Customers' Notes held as margin,	646.42	662.49	4,305.35
DEFICIENCY, as stated on page 2 of this,		93,849.11	
Deduct, increased valuation of Mortgage			
on *Greater N. Y. lots* assigned in 18.. to			
Mother-in-law at $1,000 and included by			
debtor in his statement of 15th JANU-			
ARY 18.. as $700, difference,		300.00	93,549.11

It may be possible that some value may be recovered from preferred creditors, to whom property was transferred in excess of the amount due to them, and also from the *Nat'l Bank of Deposit*, who hold Cash Balance and Notes as security for protest fees and other contingencies, incidental to maturing notes discounted by them, particulars of which cannot as yet be stated until an accounting is received from the Bank.

To give clear and complete expression of the disposition of the debtor's assets and subsequent receipts between 15th JAN. and 18th JUNE we present the following digest :

DEBTOR'S SETTLEMENT WITH RELATIVES AND FRIENDS, SHOWING AMOUNT DUE TO EACH ON 15TH JANUARY 18.. AND VALUE GIVEN SUBSEQUENTLY IN PAYMENT.

Name.	Amt. due 15th JAN. 18..	Subsequent Payments.
Mother-in-law,	$11,000.00	$3,600.00
Brother,	24,812.40	28,000.00
Brother-in-law, b.	11,208.75	9,065.60
Confidential Salesman,	2,565.95	3,589.35
Brother-in-law, a.	8,500.48	8,500.48
" Customers' Notes,	274.75	274.75
Wife,	2,487.20	
Insolvent Debtor's private bills,	496.04	496.04
	61,345.57	53,526.22

DEBTOR'S SETTLEMENT WITH GENERAL CREDITORS, SHOWING AMOUNT DUE AT 15TH JANUARY 18.., INCREASED BY SUBSEQUENT PURCHASES, AND AMOUNT PAID ON ACCOUNT, AND BALANCE REMAINING UNPAID.

On 15th JAN., 18.., LIABILITIES as stated by debtor,		$120,699.32	
Add *Creditors' a/c* omitted but subsequently paid,		1.00	$120.700.32
Deduct Accounts due Relatives and Friends, per preceding page,		61,345.57	
Balance due on Notes and Open Accounts to General Creditors, 15th JAN. 18..,			$59,354.75
Add Subsequent purchases on open *a/c*,			40,432.78
Total indebtedness to General Creditors,			99,787.53
Payments on acct. of indebtedness prior to 15th JAN. 18 ,			
Customers' Notes given, see page 18 of this,	5,422.72		
" " returned, and interest,	4,814.37	608.35	
Cash and Mdse, payments on *a/c*,	15,483.01		
Deduct Loans by General Creditors to retire old Notes, *Dry Creditor*, 329.80			
Dry Creditor, 2,000.00	2,329.80		
Actual payments, see page 21 of this,		13,153.21	
Total Payments on acct., 15th JAN. 18.. indebtedness,		13,761.56	
Payments on acct. of indebtedness contracted subsequent to 15th JAN. 18.., Cash and Mdse, as per page 21 of this,		556.67	
Total Value paid on account*,			14,318.23
			85,469.30
Add Amount due to Customers for over-payment,		22.00	
Add Amount due from Creditors for over-payment,		7.55	29.55
*included in above payments and herewith cancelled			
LIABILITIES TO GENERAL CREDITORS, 18TH JUNE 18..			
On Open Account, per Schedule on page 19 of this,		29,106.17	
On Bills Payable, per Schedule on page 20 of this,		56,392.68	85,498.85

DISPOSITION OF ASSETS, IN HAND 15TH JAN. 18.. AND THEREAFTER ACQUIRED BY PURCHASE AND FROM OTHER SOURCES.

To Asset value in hand 15th JAN. 18.. as per debtor's statement,		$39,128.16	
To Purchases from General Creditors, subsequent to 15th JAN. 18..,		40,432.78	
To Difference in value, Mtg. on Lots, assigned value,	$1,000.00		
Ledger value,	700.00	300.00	
To Net Increase value realized subsequent to 15th JAN. 18.., as per Deficiency Acct.,		1,364.31	
To Amount overpaid by Customers,	22.00		
" " " to Creditors, *	7.55	29.55	$81,254.80

DISPOSITION.

By Payments to Relatives and Friends on claims prior to 15th JAN. 18..,		53,526.22	
By Payments to General Creditors, on claims prior to 15th JAN. 18..,		13,761.56	
By Payments to General Creditors, on claims after 15th JAN. 18..		556.67	
By Losses on Sales,		731.07	
By Expenses Selling Goods and Factory Rent,		3,286.50	
By General Expenses, etc. (deducting Interest $1,007.60 included in $53,526.22),		1,678.14	
By *Insolvent Debtor*, Personal Drawings for 5 mos.		6,937.95	80,478.11
By BALANCE, *Brother-in-law*, a. amt. paid 12th April, 18..,	114.20		
National Bank of Deposit, held as margin,	662.49		776.69

The foregoing concludes a simple recital of the figures arrived at after an investigation of the debtor's books, and which have been proven to be accurate by a rigid application of the principles of double entry, analysis and controlling accounts, and can be supported in every particular by detailed working sheets in our possession, and while the data submitted has been imperfect and scattered, the painstaking care that has been expended upon the work warrants us in pronouncing our figures substantially correct, and the deductions made therefrom and the methods and obvious purposes of the debtor, as revealed by his accounts and herinafter stated by us, to be facts unquestionable and easily demonstrated, viz:—

That the debtor was aware of his insolvency at 15th Jan. 18..

That his condition had been growing worse during the following year.

That there was no chance of regaining his solvency at 15th JAN. 18..

That in order to prefer his relatives and friends, it would be necessary to fraudulently obtain the necessary funds, by subsequently purchasing heavily without any provision for paying for the goods, and selling without any design for profit, below cost, to persons of indifferent credit, assuming heavy expenses for salesmen's commissions and traveling expenses, and in short, converting the goods into cash at any sacrifice, and *that he did so.*

That between 15th JAN and 18th JUNE 18.., (5 mos.) he purchased merchandise to the amount of $40,432.78.

That he paid on account of said merchandise only $556.67.

That between 15th JAN. and 18th JUNE 18.., (5 mos.) he sold goods amounting to $33,892.71 for $731.07 less than the purchase price and cost of manufacture.

That in effecting such sales he incurred an additional loss in salesmen's commissions, salaries, and traveling expenses of $3,286.50.

That between 15th JAN. and 18th JUNE 18.., (5 mos.) his current business losses were $5,972.24.

That his personal drawings for 5 months between 15th JAN. and 18th JUNE 18.. were $6,937.95.

That according to the debtor's own testimony his personal drawings for previous years averaged $7,000 to $7,500 for each year.

That he owed his relatives and friends on 15th JAN. 18.. $61,345.57.

That at 15th JAN. 18.. the debtor's gross Assets were only $31,128.16.

That after sustaining a subsequent loss of $5,972.24 he paid to his relatives and friends between 15th JAN. and 18th JUNE 18.. the sum of $53,526.22:

That at 15th JAN. 18.. he owed the General Creditors $59,354.75.

That all he has since paid to the general creditors on the aforesaid amount is $13,761.56.

That he has not since 15th JAN. 18.. incurred any additional indebtedness to his relatives and friends which was not almost immediately
repaid.

That he now owes his general creditors $85,498.85, of which
$39,876.11 was incurred subsequent to 15th JAN. 18.. and all of which
remains due and unpaid.

That no available assets remain.

That the indebtedness to his *Brother* was with interest $25,494.74
and that he delivered to him merchandise to the value of $28,000.00, an
overpayment of $2,505.26, and that he made no entry upon his books of
such delivery of goods.

BROTHER-IN-LAW, a.   The transactions of the debtor with this
firm afford a specific instance of the method by which his relatives and
friends were preferred at the expense of the general creditors, and by
value fraudulently obtained from the latter to accomplish the act.

From the Account Current rendered by *Brother-in-law a.* and submitted
to us, and from the books of the debtor, the dealings between these
parties are disclosed as follows:

The balance due by the debtor to *Brother-in-law a.* at 1st Jan.
  (2 yrs. since), representing purchases made in previous
  year and as per their Acct. Current is, $17,574.17

On 19th Jan. (same yr.) the debtor sold them goods in amount $1,588.50

" 24th "   "   "   . "   "   7,358.60

  It is to be noted that these sales were made immediately after the day upon which it was customary for Mr.
Debtor to take stock and ascertain his financial condition,
and as we know that it was unfavorable, the expediency
of covering *Brother-in-law's a/c* is apparent.

On 13th Sep. (next yr.) the debtor sold them goods in amount   269.12

" 11th Dec.   "   "   "   "   165.34   9,381.56

                                                   8,192.61

With the exception of above entries the account comprises Note and
Cash transactions with interest, all of which liquidate with the exception of a Balance at 15 JAN., 18.., of $8,500.48, which comprises the
above balance of $8,192.61 and unsettled part of interest.

In part settlement of this latter account the debtor purchased from
Contesting Creditor on 8th April, 18.., Mdse. amounting to $2,544.15 and

these same goods were immediately delivered to *Brother-in-Law, a.*, but were not charged up as a cash sale until 30 April, 18.., the entry then being crowded into the sales book on page 102, apparently after the sales book had been in use for May sales. These goods were billed to *Brother-in-Law, a.*, at the cost price less four per cent., resulting in a loss of $101 75. *Brother-in-Law* a. paid the bill on 30 April, 18.., as appears by cash book entry on folio 42 as a cash sale No entry, however, of either sale or settlement appears on *Brother-in-Law's a.* account, although the cheque thus received from *Brother-in-Law, a.* was duly deposited in the *National Bank of Deposit.* The debtor then issued his cheque under date of 1st May 18.. to *Brother-tn-Law, a.* for $2,500, which amount was charged to *Brothe-in-Law's a.* account, giving the appearance of a cash payment on account, whereas, in point of fact, it was a payment in merchandise obtained from *Contesting Creditor*, without any intention of paying for the same, and turned over to *Brother-in-Law, a.* at a loss of $101.75, and the only purpose of treating it as a Cash Sale and receiving *Brother-in-Law's a.* cheque therefor, and then paying a cheque to *Brother-in-Law, a.* in a perfunctory manner for a slightly larger amount, was solely to cloak a transaction obviously fraudulent upon its face.

In the debtor's examination under oath (see page 12, examinations on 26th August. 18..) he states that these goods were sold at a profit.

With the exception of $1,181.63 of Customers' Notes given *Brother-in-Law, a.* in further part settlement, the remainder of the settlement which appears on the Ledger as having been made in cash, in like manner to the foregoing transaction, was, in fact, identical in nature to the total extent of $8,542.50 merchandise cash sales, all of which were disguised in the same manner by receiving from and paying to *Brother-in-Law, a.* cheques therefor, to maintain the appearance of cash settlements upon the Ledger, as is more fully shown by the analysis of *Brother-in-Law's, a.* account on page 26 of this.

Brother-in-Law's, a. firm were evidently in the debtor's confidence as to his condition, and although sustaining intimate and friendly connection, had sold the Debtor no goods for three years past, but the greater part of the settlements since seem to have been in goods received from the debtor at, so far as we can trace. BELOW COST PRICE, and it is difficult to understand how an importing house should buy in that manner from a local jobber who should normally be a purchaser from them, without the unavoidable conclusion that they were conspirators in advising, aiding and abetting so *successful a failure*.

We note that in addition to the settlement of *Brother-in-Law's*, a. account, the bebtor paid them on 12th April $114.20, for which no consideration can be traced, neither does it appear in the account current submitted to us.

INSOLVENT DEBTOR. In addition to the cheques of $2,500.00 and $200.00 drawn by the debtor just prior to his European trip, the disposition of which has been testified to by him, it appears that other cash receipts amounting to $711.72 and comprising the last few entries in the Cash Book were not deposited in the bank and neither has the debtor accounted for their disposition. The items aggregating this amount we have charged to his account, a complete statement of which appears on pages 23-25.

Following we append accounts in support of the foregoing statements and to which reference has been made and which can readily be found by means of the index preceding this report.

Faithfully yours,

Broaker & Chapman.

HEREDITARY INSOLVENCY.

Contesting Creditor, and another

vs.   } Accountants' Report.

Insolvent Debtor, et al.

Messrs. *Contesting Creditors*,

No. .. Cliff Street, New York.

Dear Sirs:

We submit herewith the results of our examination of the books of Messrs. *Insolvent Debtors* for the period of fourteen months and four days, commencing 15th May, 18.., and ending 18th July, 18.., the latter date being at or about the date of the failure and subsequent to which no further entries appear upon their financial books.

The books with which our investigation has chiefly to deal are the Ledger, Sales Book, and Cash Book, and while many items in the two latter books have not been posted, we have included all such items in our accounting, by allocating them to, and blending them with the Ledger accounts affected, together with such items appearing upon the assignee's schedules, which, although not appearing upon the books, were proper subjects of entry and necessary to be considered, at the same time disallowing and expunging from the assignee's schedule such items as are of a personal nature and foreign to the actual business as indicated by their financial books, in which they in no wise appear.

CHEQUE BOOKS AND BANK PASS BOOKS.

Our examination of the Cheque Books and Bank Pass Books submitted to us, rendered it at once apparent that in no sense could they be properly regarded as account books of the business we were investigating, any more than the private pockets of individuals remotely connected with it, for, in addition to containing records of the Bank lodgements of funds in part receipts of the business in question and payments by cheque constituting disbursements of the business in question, they were replete with items or parts of items, both as to deposit and cheque, in no wise affecting the business and relating to the receipt of moneys which the business proper never received, and constituting the proceeds arising from assets the business never possessed, and payments of money in settlement of liabilities that never appeared upon the financial books, and representing in many instances investments in or charges to property never ranked as an asset of the business and not listed among the assets in the assignee's schedule. Had we been supplied with the deposit slips we requested, the cheque books would have afforded us excellent data for tracing receipts of the business for which it may have never received credit, but we can only reiterate that they (the Cheque Books and Bank Pass Books) can no more be regarded as being part of the account books of the business than the private bank account of any individual containing scattered items of a business he was indirectly connected with, could be regarded as the account books of said business, *and the stress that has been laid by Messrs. Attorneys for the Insolvent Debtors upon the specific identity of these cheques and pass books with the business before us, in preference even to the financial books applying exclusively to said business, is utterly untenable.*

BALANCE SHEET.

Referring to our Balance Sheet on page — of this it is thereon shown that the books were opened to show a *prima facie* balance to the credit of Messrs. *Insolvent Debtors* as net capital investment of $11,852.90, whereas in point of fact (admitting the propriety of including in the assignee's schedules the notes and loans of $35,560.16, and having regard for the fact that said loans omitted from the liabilities, and since in part liquidated, must have been at the time considerably larger in amount), there was a capital deficit, and the opening of the books with a statement so willfully false, was at the outset a fraud upon any creditor or subsequent investor who might have had occasion to rely upon the statements appearing upon the firm's books.

MR. SHARP.

The investment of $20,000 by *Mr. Sharp* (while in reality only about $16,900, but entered by request of " ? " at the former amount, as per sworn testimony of Mr. *Iusolvent Debtor, A.*), although now construed by him as a loan, bears all the appearance and characteristics of an investment for gain or loss of an incoming partner, and from all that we can discover after a critical inquiry into the facts, we are firm in our opinion that the consideration (for said loan) of a third interest in patents pending (still vested in him) and the further security of a mortgage on Real Estate (at the time standing in the name of *Insolvent Debtor, A.* during his father's embarrassments, and now ostensibly the property of the father during his son's embarrassments), together with the discreet withholding of the loan from the assignee's schedule of liabilities is but a well conceived conspiracy to defraud the creditors, and place *Mr. Sharp* beyond the reach of his liability to the general creditors, with his investment intact as a sort of compensation for the misstatement of actual condition at the time he invested the $16,900 aforesaid.

TRADING AND PROFIT AND LOSS ACCOUNT.

We have prepared a Trading and Profit and Loss Account to which your attention is specially called. It is presented in two sections. The first or Trading section corresponds to the Manufacturing Account in the Ledger and deals with the Prime Cost, including Material and Labor, as against the Proceeds from Sales, showing an excess of cost over proceeds, or Trading loss of $7,669.38, to which is added in the second or Profit and Loss section the Management Expense, Interest, Insurance, etc., which swell the total losses for the period under review to the sum of $25,066.51. This arrangement, being carried out on the same lines in which the Revenue is stated on their books, admits of perfect comparison with the state of the account as shown at any previous date within the period reviewed and brings at once to our notice the somewhat startling fact that their Manufacturing Account (of which our Trading Account is a continuation and completion), showed at 2nd June (latter year) a

Profit . . . . . . (see Ledger pages 46 and 54) of .	$1,255.17
From which deducting the discounts, " " 12 and 54) of . .	867.40
Would still leave a Trading Profit of	$387.77

arising from business transactions covering about 13 months, whereas at
  the date of the failure, only 48 days subsequent, the Trading Account
  dealing identically with the same elements shows a loss of . . $7,669.38

Showing a loss sustained during the last 48 days' business of . . $8,057.15

and resulting from a volume of business involving only about $16,000 of recorded sales. This is without reference in both cases to the management expenses, interest, insurance, etc., which are held separate and apart both upon their books and upon our statements.

This abnormal loss on Trading during the short time preceding their failure, immediately suggests inquiry into possible causes which are anything but assurances of good faith. Our attention has been called to a sale, the proceeds from which were deposited in the bank, but for which the business never received credit on its books, amounting to $174.93, paid by *Mr. Customer*, and we have no way of ascertaining how many more accidental or willful omissions of sales may have been made, in which the money did *not* go in the bank but was simply pocketed. The inventory handed over to the assignee might also be increased, if made to include valuable lots of goods in part or whole completed, in the custody of various workmen numbering over one hundred, and quietly resting in hiding places until the breeze blows over, and a little detective work on these lines might not be ill-directed. What we feel confident in asserting is, that the losses during the last 48 days are out of all proportion to the volume of business done, and we would recommend a critical examination of the comparative cost and proceeds of every sale during that period, which, if not indicating a wanton slaughter in prices, would confirm the suspicion that there is something radically wrong in the amount of unsold stock delivered to the assignee.

GENERAL REMARKS.

We regret our inability to separate in detail the bank transactions applying to the business from those which were extraneous, as also to trace the note transactions, and report upon the separate loans from *Mrs. Wife* and *Credulity & Co.*; but in order to do so it was essential that we should have had the deposit slips of the several Bank Accounts, which we requested and were unable to obtain.

We note that the Consignment Account of *Credulity & Co.*, on Ledger page 71, shows a Dr. balance in ink of $693.52 left standing as a live asset, across which is written "this account is worth about $100." In view of the fact that *Credulity & Co.* are creditors upon the Ledger for $98.98, and for a further sum of $5,000 not appearing upon the Ledger, the omission of the Dr. account and failure to rank it against the liability to the same party, impresses us as a fact warranting inquiry on the part of the general creditors.

The payment by *Insolvent Debtor, A.*, to his father (see testimony on page 77), of from $15,000 to $24,000 yearly as the net revenue (after paying taxes, repairs, and interest on mortgages) from Real Estate worth only $98,000 (see testimony, pages 70 and 76), and mortgaged up to the limit, impresses us as a phenomenally large income under the most favorable circumstances.

Faithfully yours,

Broaker & Chapman.

(See Balance Sheet and Profit and Loss Acct. following on pages 172, 173, 174 and 175).

BALANCE SHEET—INSOLVENT

CASH	on hand. Deposited in Union Bank,		$4 04	
	Leather "		2 18	
	German "		21 50	$27 72
MERCHANDISE,	Inventory of Goods, etc., as taken from Assignee's Schedule. See Schedule A on page 11 of this,			9,933 65
MACHINERY,	Balance as per Ledger folio 64,		22,214 89	
	Payable Book Debts as taken from Assignee's Schedule but not appearing upon the books. Per Schedule D.(2) on page 16 of this,		209 20	22,424 09
	(*Note,*--This Account includes Furniture and Fixtures. See Schedule B (a) (b) on pages 12-14 of this.)			
PATENTS.	Balance as per Ledger folio 26.			1,691 25
BOOK DEBTS RECEIVABLE.	as per schedule C on page 15 of this,			711 25
	ASSETS. (Upon basis of a going business).....................		....	34,787 96
JOHN BROWN.	Payment of Note as per Schedule H on page 25 of this,		1,50 00	
CASH.	Amount of Taxes and other charges deducted by Mr. Sharp from loan of $20,000 as per written statement pinned on page 55 of Cash Book.			
	(Full amount of $20,000 Cr. contra),		3,100 00	
WORKMEN'S DEPOSITS.	As stated in Assignee's Schedule but not entered in Cash Book as per Schedule E on page 21,		95 00	
PROFIT AND LOSS ACCOUNT.	Loss on Trading,	$7,669.38		
	Expenses, etc.,	17,397.13		
	as per Profit and Loss Acct., page 718,		25,066 51	
	CAPITAL DRAWINGS, LOSSES AND EXPENSES,			29,761 51
				64 549 47

EXPENDITURES MADE BY INSOLVENT DEBTORS

jointly or severally in liquidating unstated liabilities or making investments, prior and subsequent to 15th May 18--, but in no wise appearing upon their business accounts, although necessarily equivalent in amount to the complementary liabilities stated contra,

	35,560 16
	35,560 16

DEBTORS AS AT 18TH JULY, 18—.

Book Debts Payable	as per Schedule D (1) on page 16 of this,		$28,674 44
" " "	as taken from Assignee's Schedules,		
Sundry Machinery Bills,	per Schedule D (2), page 16,	$209 20	
" Manufacturing "	" " D (3), " 16,	1,308 65	
" Labor "	" " E ("), " 21,	2,140 68	
" Workmen's Deposits,	" " " ("), " 21,	95 00	3,753 53

Liabilities		....	32,427 97
Capital, L. fo. 1 (combined),	Insolvent Debtors as of 15th May, 18—,	11,852 90	
Mr. Sharp.	Cash received from him and expended in the business, stated as a loan against ⅓ interest in Patents, and additionally secured by Mortgage on Real Estate not included in Assignee's Schedules of Assets (see $3,100 contra),	20,000 00	
Cash.	Amount (approximate) entered in Cash Book, page 2, in excess of amount received, $3,100.00		
	Amount Bank Balances handed Assignee, 27.72		
	3,127.72		
	Deduct Cash Balance Dr. on page 54 of C. B., 2,859.12		
	Difference invested in business from outside sources,	268 60	
Capital.	including Investments subsequent to 15 May, 18--,		32,121 50
			64,549 47

Liabilities Included in Assignee's Schedules,
but not appearing upon the books and incurred prior and subsequent to 15th May, 18—

Credulity & Co.,	as per Schedule D (4), on page 16,	5,000 00	
Peter Jones,	" " " D (5), " " 16,	2,831 66	
Sundry Notes and Loans,	" " " D (6), " " 17,	23,728 50	

Liabilities Not Included in Assignee's Schedules,
nor appearing upon Insolvent Debtor's Books,

Mrs. Wife,	as per Schedule D (7) on page 17.	4,000 00	35,560 16

DR.   TRADING AND PROFIT AND LOSS ACCOUNT OF

To INVENTORY.	(as of 15th May, 18—,) as per Ledger folio 4,			$11,077 9I
" SUNDRY PURCHASES.	as per Ledger folio 75 and Schedule F on page 23 of of this,	$33,452 55		
	as per Ledger folio 75 and Schedule G on page 24 of this,	654 84	34,107 39	
" LABOR.	as per Ledger folio 75 and Schedule I on page 26 of this,	58,976 94		
	Unposted Items in Cash Book per Schedule H on page 25 of this,	7,873 71		
	Unpaid Bills per Assignee's Schedule and Schedule E on page 21 of this,	2,140 68	68,991 33	
" EXPENSES (Manuf'g.).	as per Ledger folio 75 and Schedule I on page 26 of this,	5,131 18		
	Unposted items in Cash Book per Schedule H on page 25 of this,	136 88		
	Unpaid Bills per Assignee's Schedule and Schedule D on page 16 of this,	1,308 65	6,576 71	
			120,753 34	
	Deduct,			
	DISCOUNTS (allowed by —) as per Led. fol. 12,	146 26		
	INVENTORY (18 July, 18—,) per Assignee's Schedule,	9,933 65	10,079 91	
	PRIME COST.............................		110,673 43	
			110.673 43	
To BALANCE	brought down,		7,669 38	
" INTEREST,	as per Led. fol. 12, ·		355 00	
" INSURANCE,	" " " " 5,		315 00	
" EXPENSES AND DRAWINGS,	inextricably mixed, per Expense Acct. Led. fol. 53 and Schedule J on page 30 of this,	13,812 98		
	Unposted Items in Cash Book per Schedule H on page 25 of this,	1,714 15	15,527 13	
" ATTORNEY FOR INSOLVENT DEBTORS.	unposted item in Cash Book per Schedule H on page 25 of this,		1,200 00	
			$25,066 51	

INSOLVENT DEBTOR 15th May, 18—, to 18th July, 18—, (14 mos.) CR.

By Sales	on Credit per Ledger fol. 75,		$98,383 50	
" "	Cash, " " " "		250 84	
" "	on Credit, " Sales Book, page 323,	$6,466.71		
	add error,	.50	6,467 21	
	as per page 27 of this, Schedule J,			$105,101 55
	Deduct,			
Discounts on Sales per Led. fol. 12 and Schedule K,			724 84	
Rebates " " " " " 75 " G,			949 70	
Returns " " " " " 75 " L,			422 96	2,097 50
Proceeds				103,004 05
By Balance, being excess of Cost over Proceeds, carried down,				7,669 38
				110,673 43
By Balance, being Losses and Drawings, undistinguishable, carried to Balance Sheet on pages——,				25,066 51
				$25,066 51

SCOPE OF ACCOUNTANCY.

THE SCOPE OF ACCOUNTANCY
AND
THE QUALIFICATIONS OF AN ACCOUNTANT,
WITH
NOTES ON ACCOUNTANCY LITERATURE.

The title by which the Professional Accountant generally designates himself in those sections where accountancy has not, as yet, become legally recognized as a profession, is "Public Accountant and Auditor," and while the distinguishing titles of "Certified Public Accountant" (C.P.A.) in the State of New York, and "Chartered Accountant" (F.C.A.) in Great Britain, convey the further idea of qualification under the law and consequent greater assurance of personal fitness, the title "Public Accountant and Auditor" still remains the most comprehensive designation of the profession.

This title at once suggests the two principal kinds of work that devolve upon the Professional Accountant, namely—(1) the work of an *Accountant*, and (2) the work of an *Auditor;* and while the capacity to perform both of such kinds of service rests upon education and experience, identical in nature and simultaneously acquired, they are, nevertheless, separate and distinct classes of work, and in the performance of each the Accountant fulfills a separate and distinct function.

The work of the *Accountant* is *creative*, while that of the *Auditor* is *inspective*.

The function of the Accountant is to design and organize systems
of accounts, conduct or superintend the operation thereof, determine and
adjust the interests of the parties concerned (whether sole trader, firm
or corporation), and draft entries properly recording the same, giving
clear expression to the facts, upon opening the accounts at the commencement or reorganization of an undertaking, or at the close of its
fiscal periods or final liquidation.

The function of an Auditor is to review and critically examine
accounts which are complete, or presumably so, at the date to which his
audit extends.

We cite an instance of a forwarding agency in New York, whose
books were required to be audited annually by a resident Chartered
Accountant appointed by the home office in London, in which case the
said Chartered Accountant refused to enter upon the audit until a
difference then existing in the Trial Balance was located and corrected.

This difference in the Trial Balance baffled the efforts of the agency's
book-keepers for several weeks, during which time the Accountant
appointed by the home office held aloof, and not until the error had been
located and corrected, by other Accountants called in at the private
expense of the local manager, did the Chartered Accountant enter upon
his audit.

We fail to understand why the Chartered Accountant did not engage
to find the error and so make the additional fee, which in this case was
larger than he received for his audit, although he was technically correct
in refusing to perform such service as part of the audit, without further
compensation; the books being manifestly incorrect were not in condition
to receive an auditor's attention until their mathematical accuracy, at
least, was established.

In another instance, an accountant, in the course of an audit, discovered an error which threw the books out of the apparent balance they
were in when he entered upon his work. He called the attention of the
firm to the matter, and explained to them that as he had engaged to
audit the accounts for a fixed fee he could not be expected to locate
treacherous differences, and he would have to discontinue the audit
until they located the contra error; if they chose, however, to have him
locate it he would agree to find it for an additional fee. They accepted

his proposition, and as the error revealed itself subsequently in the course of the audit, the accountant made a clear gain through assuming the function of an Accountant while engaged as an Auditor.

There is still another class of work which partakes of the nature of both Accounting and Auditing, which is known under the general term "investigations." The purposes for which accountants are engaged upon this class of work are extremely varied, and occur in the course of every description of business, but as a few of the purposes stand out more prominently than the rest they may be generally classified as follows:

Investigations on behalf of incoming partners, for the purpose of ascertaining the financial condition and earning power of the businesses in which they purpose to invest.

Investigations on behalf of Syndicates who contemplate the purchase of industrial enterprises or other undertakings, with a view to converting them into corporations; which investigations have for their purpose the determining of the profits made during past years, the average yearly profit, the percentage of increase or decrease, the relative capital employed, and other matters which collectively form the basis of purchase price and capitalization. These investigations are often made at the instance of the vendors or promoters, and it is generally customary for the accountant, in addition to his report, to give a certificate as to profits, which certificate is frequently embodied in the published prospectus issued for the purpose of inviting public subscription to the capital stock of the undertaking.

The practice of giving certificates based solely upon working papers is a dangerous practice and the accountant who certifies to profits should also render a full and exhaustive report upon his investigation showing the processes and figures by which he has arrived at the profits certified to, and reference to such report and the date it was delivered should be embodied in the certificate, which latter should state only the bare facts concerning the past profits, without any speculative hypothesis concerning the future, and leave it entirely to the vendor in his separate statement to assume all responsibility for any flowery statements or sanguine expectations concerning future dividends held out as inducements to subscribers.

Investigations on behalf of creditors for the purpose of ascertaining the resources of an embarrassed debtor, the prospects of recovery or otherwise, the existence of fraud or unwarranted preferences in the disposition of his assets or creation of his liabilities, with a view to further extension of credit, private composition, or institution of insolvency proceedings.

Investigations of accounts on behalf of principals or others, where the same have become tangled and complicated through incompetency, mismanagement, fraud or sudden death of those who have been relied upon for their preparation or elucidation, including the accounts of public officials, firms and corporations, executors, administrators, guardians, assignees and receivers, for the purpose of untangling and straightening out complications, detecting fraud, correcting errors, and re-discovering data apparently lost, and, in short, rendering the accounts again clear, systematic and correct.

While it will be seen that *investigations*, like *audits*, consist chiefly of a review of past accounts, the accountant is not in a position to require the accounts to be free from obvious errors or in any sense complete. The books submitted to him may have been kept by single entry and it would consequently devolve upon him to create the entire nominal section, or to employ some other expedient to the end of ascertaining the profits where the same form the subject of inquiry; or the accounts may consist of the crudest memoranda and call for a complete re-writing and revising of the entire detail, the sifting of evidence and employment of the processes of allocation, analysis, synthesis, tabulation and recapitulation, involving the production of intricate and voluminous working papers, the compilation therefrom of the final statements, and the preparation of the report.

The work of an Accountant covers a broad field and it is difficult to bring the almost infinite variety of business undertakings with which it has to deal under any but the most elastic classification. It includes every degree of book-keeping, from the simplest detail to the construction of the most elaborate systems, and comprehends the entire range of business and financial considerations from the duties of an entry clerk in a Counting House to the system, organization and direction of the National Exchequer.

However, there are certain specific lines of accountancy work which form the specialties of certain Professional Accountants or constitute the greater part of their practice and have accordingly gained prominence and seem to form classifications under which the work naturally falls, to wit:—

Mercantile and Manufacturing Accounting, relating to the accounts of traders and manufacturers. This classification includes shipping and commission merchants, importers, jobbers, retailers, brokers, and concerns engaged in manufacturing of every description, and comprehends, by far, the greatest variety and extent of business enterprise.

Transportation and Common Carriers' Accounting, relating to the accounts of steamships, railroads, express companies, telegraph companies, telephone companies, water companies, gas companies and electric light companies.

Mining Accounting, relating to the accounts of the companies engaged in the mining of gold, silver, copper, tin, lead, iron and other ores, coal, salt, borax, mineral oils and similar natural products.

Publication Accounting, relating to the accounts of houses engaged in the printing, publishing and sale of books, magazines and periodicals, the accounts of newspapers and trade journals, advertising agencies, and trade bureaus, news companies, etc.

Financial Accounting, relating to the accounts of banks, trust companies, insurance companies, surety companies, title guarantee companies, building loan associations, and similar institutions.

Fiduciary Accounting, relating to the accounts of executors, administrators, guardians, trustees, assignees, and receivers, with respect to systematizing their accounts in such manner as to afford ready data for preparing schedules and accountings for filing in the Surrogates' and other Courts, and the preparation of said accounts in prescribed legal forms.

Public Accounting, relating to the accounts of the National Government, State, County and City Exchequers, and subordinate bureaus and departments.

Miscellaneous Accounting, relating to the accounts of hotels, hospitals, asylums, churches, friendly societies, clubs, trade unions, associations, and a variety of other accounts coming under no particular classification.

From the foregoing brief review of the function of the "Public Accountant and Auditor" and the varied classes of business undertakings he is called upon to equip with systems of accounts and methodize in their procedure, as also to certify to the correctness of the results indicated by their books of account after making audit thereof, it is obvious that the education and experience of a Public Accountant should be both liberal and extended, and some few remarks upon the facilities that exist for acquiring the technical education and practical experience which directly appertain to a competent and successful practice in this profession, will here be in keeping.

The fundamental education, apart from general scholarship, should be a thorough knowledge of double entry book-keeping and business routine, and besides numerous commercial schools of various degrees of excellence, in some instances maintaining a very satisfactory standard, there are to be had in the United States many text-books on book-keeping, both those in use in the commercial schools and others published for general sale. These works, however, with few exceptions, do not go beyond what we would term "the school course", and while being replete with working exercises admirably designed to qualify the student for entering a Counting House, after he has grown proficient by supplemental experience in the simple duties of his position and become a fairly intelligent book-keeper he can find nothing in them to take him beyond or lift him out of the mechanical groove in which he is running. While he may move smoothly in the line of his duties and understand, well enough for all intents and purposes, the accounts of the business in which he has been trained, his experience of each day becomes but a repetition of the day before, and consequently the *broad principles of accountancy*, that are all-pervading and limited to no particular conditions or environments, and the *logical grasp of generalities* and *faculty of applying radical principles* without any difficulty attendant upon change of detail no matter of how novel a nature, that characterize the capacity and achievements of a Public Accountant, are to the book-keeper a sealed book, to be opened only by means of a broader field of experience together with extended reading of technical literature emanating from the minds of Accountants high in their profession and written for the express purpose of assisting each other in the abstract conception and facile application of those essential principles which have been and are constantly being evolved and developed in higher accountancy.

Referring to the text-books treating with the fundamental principles of book-keeping and designed for beginners, there are many excellent works to be had and among some which have come to our notice and which we feel warranted in recommending are the following works:

New Complete Book-keeping, by Williams & Rogers, published by E. R. Andrews, Rochester, N. Y.

The Canadian Accountant, Book-keeping, by L. G. Beatty and J.W. Johnson, F.C.A., Ontario Business College, Belleviile, Ontario, Canada.

The New Bryant and Stratton Counting House Book-keeping, by S. S. Packard and H. B. Bryant, published by Ivison, Blakeman, Taylor & Co., New York and Chicago.

These books are published expressly for use in business colleges.

Another class of works which are published for more general dissemination and have been extensively advertised are:

Keister's Corporation Accounting and Auditing, by D. A. Keister, 98 Euclid Ave., Cleveland, Ohio.

Soule's New Science and Practice of Accounts, by George Soule, 603 St. Charles St., New Orleans, Louisiana.

Goodwin's improved Book-Keeping and Business Manual, by J. H. Goodwin, 1215 Broadway, New York.

These latter works, in addition to treating with the subject of book-keeping, contain an extensive and valuable compilation of *commercial law* and *business forms*. The style in which they are written, however, as well as the manner in which they are advertised, strikes us as being somewhat sensational, and as their treatment of many accountancy subjects does not accord with the treatment for which we have a preference, we are disposed to let them rest upon their own merits believing that, if read advisedly, there is much useful information to be gained, and the energy and patience which are displayed in their compilation is beyond question.

Coming now to the subject of *technical literature*, by which term we mean the works of Professional Accountants written for *the profession*, we have to confess that no such works of any prominence, published in the United States, have come to our notice.   There have, indeed, been works claiming to be of such character, which upon examination show that they were written merely to sell, and while running into high page numbers and treating in an imaginary sort of way with a variety of businesses, contain but a repetition of simple detail under different names, and altogether fail to realize the stupendous hopes excited by the promises contained in their voluminous indices.

We are therefore compelled to go abroad for high grade technical literature, and happily we find that which we are seeking in the accountancy literature of Great Britain, where for years past the profession has occupied an exalted plane, attracted to itself the finest intellects, and developed a galaxy of writers of marked ability.

We would, therefore, (without disparaging in any sense the national pride we feel in American Accountants, coming ourselves from old American stock, and having every confidence in their literary ability and native genius, when they are established to an equal degree with their English cousins), earnestly recommend to the student of accountancy who desires to profit by the best accountancy literature extant to procure the following English works:

Auditing.   A Practical Manuel for Auditors, by Lawrence R. Dicksee, F. C. A., of the firm of Price and Dicksee, formerly lecturer on Book-keeping at the Technical Schools of the County Burrough of Cardiff.

Factory Accounts, their Principles and Practice.   A Handbook for Accountants and Manufacturers, by Emile Garke and J. M. Fells.

THE ACCOUNTANTS' MANUAL.

Questions set at the Institute of Chartered Accountants' Examinations, with answers thereto, together with copious index.

Vol.   I, from December, 1884, to June 1887, both inclusive.
Vol. II,   "   "   1887, "   "   1890,   "   "
Vol. III,   "   "   1890, "   "   1892,   "   "
Vol. IV,   "   "   1892, "   "   1894,   "   "
Vol. V,   "   "   1894, "   "   1896,   "   "

Textile Manufacturers' Book-keeping, for Counting House, Mill and Warehouse. Being a practical treatise specially designed for the Woolen,

Worsted and Allied Trades; by George Pepler Norton. A. C. A., of the firm of Armatage & Norton, Chartered Accountants, of Kudersfield and Dewsbury.

Railway Accounts and Finance. An Exposition of the Principles and Practice of Railway Accounting in all its branches, by J. Alfred Fisher.

Newspaper Accounts. Being a practical treatise on the Books and Accounts in use in large and small Newspaper Offices, by Benjamin T. Norton, F. C. A., and George T..Feasey, A. C. A., of the firm of Pratt & Norton, 9 Old Jewelry Chambers, London.

The Accountant's and Book-keeper's Vade Mecum. A series of short and concise articles upon Capital and Revenue Expenditure, Revenue Accounts, Depreciation, Reserve and Sinking Funds, Adjustment of Partnership Accounts and Tabular Book-keeping, by G. E. Stewart Whatley (Accountant Examiner, Institute Chartered Accountants).

The Accountant. A weekly publication established in 1874 and containing among other articles the lectures delivered from time to time before the Chartered Accountants Students' Societies throughout Great Britain.

Two other works that we would recommend are, The New Commercial Law, a practical text book, by Williams and Rogers, published by E. R. Andrews, Rochester, N. Y.; and Fay's Executors', Administrators' and Guardians' Manual, a guide to proceedings in Surrogates' Courts in the State of New York, by Joseph D. Fay, published by Baker, Voorhies & Co., 66 Nassau Street, New York.

To the student who contemplates entering the profession of Public Accountant, we would emphasize the importance of practical experience going hand-in-hand with diligent study, and the necessity of several years' service on the staff of a Public Accountant, in conjunction with a carefully selected course of reading.

For while it will require an amount of studious application, well digested by after reflection before he can become eligible for such a position, he will never acquire that sense of authority, assurance, ease, tact, and engaging address so necessary to command respect in the important commissions he will be placed upon and which are only born of conscious ability repeatedly demonstrated and established, until he has actually been "under fire" and has aoquired the instincts and capabilities of a general by actual "service in the field."

It is an accountant's oft repeated experience to engage in accountancy work relating to classes of business with which he is totally unfamiliar, but if he be a man of the proper sinew it will occasion him no confusion, the details and their various characteristics are but so many *facts* which he has only to see in order to understand, while the principles governing all accounts of which he is master are as easily applied to one set of facts and conditions as to another, and he immediately becomes, with respect to the treatment and elucidation of the accounts before him, the master of the clerks and book-keepers who have been engaged upon the routine work for years, and his superiority to them is speedily made apparent.

At this point we cannot do better than quote from Mr. Dicksee's work on "Auditing," as follows:—

"THE AUDITOR'S QUALIFICATIONS.—Upon this point a considerable quantity of professional literature already exists. The subject has been touched upon in almost every presidential address delivered since the foundation of the Institute and its various local offshoots. It is not, therefore, proposed to consider the subject at any great length (for, there being no essential difference of opinion upon the matter, such a course appears to be uncalled for), but rather to briefly indicate the qualities that go to make an efficient and a successful Auditor.

"First, then, it is very generally conceded that an exhaustive knowledge of every department of book-keeping is the very A B C of the Auditor's art.

"Second in importance, probably, lies a thorough acquaintance with various statutes regulating the different undertakings in which the Auditor may be concerned.

"Thirdly, although this point has been bitterly contested by some, a sufficient knowledge, not only of business generally, but of the especial way in which various particular businesses are conducted. In his presidential address at the first provincial meeting of the Institute (in October, 1886), MR. FREDERICK WHINNEY, F. C. A., clearly advocates this doctrine when he says 'No accountant can successfully carry on his practice in all the above-mentioned branches unless he is a person of considerable knowledge, skill and experience, for he must be not only acquainted with book-keeping, which is to him as the alphabet only; but, to put it very briefly, he must have some general knowledge of various trades and their customs. * * * * He ought also to have some knowledge of the practice of the Stock Exchange,' and so on. No unprejudiced person would deny the advantage of such a knowledge as is here advocated; the only question being whether a standard is not being set so high as to be virtually unattainable, and, consequently, impracticable. The reply to this is that, in accountancy as elsewhere, it is only he who aims at absolute perfection who can expect to attain even to a decent mediocrity. A complete knowledge of everything is not readily attained in three-score years and ten, and is not to be expected as the results of five years' study under articles, but the author never yet heard it seriously suggested that the standard set for the Final Examination of the Institute indicated the limit of desirable or useful knowledge. Only let the Accountant make the most of his opportunities and he will find that liquidations and bankruptcies, as well as audits, will afford him many—and he will be surprised at the amount of knowledge he can acquire, even in a short time, and, perhaps, even more astonished at the vast amount of service such knowledge will be to him in his profession.

"Lastly, but not least, may be placed those desirable qualifications of the Auditor which are not acquired by careful study, but, rather, by *living*. Tact, caution, firmness, fairness, good temper, courage, integrity, discretion, industry, judgment, patience, clear-headedness, and reliability. In short, all those qualities that go to make a good man contribute to the making of a good Accountant, while that judicious and liberal education which is involved in the single word 'culture' is most essential for all who would excel. Accountancy is a profession calling for a width and variety of knowledge to which no man has yet set the limit: the foremost Accountants are not ashamed to say that, like Epaminondas, 'they learn something in addition every day'; let us, therefore, see no shame in following their example.

"AUDIT CLERKS.—It will not be amiss, before leaving this subject, to consider very briefly the desirable qualifications of an audit clerk. Conscientiousness may be placed in the foremost rank. A large amount of uninteresting detail must inevitably form a part of the clerk's daily routine; and the fact that the greater portion of such work may generally be scamped, without any great danger of detection, affords considerable temptation, both to the naturally slow worker, and to the gentleman of elastic conscience who wishes to make a little time for himself. Reliability is the first requisite in a clerk, and the clerk who wishes to get on must endeavor to earn a reputation for being "safe." Next, the clerk would be wise—especially the young clerk—not to get too friendly with his client's staff. Let him be cautious of accepting favors, and *most* cautious of accepting presents which might easily drift into bribes. In this respect clerks may sometimes find themselves in a very difficult position (more perhaps from force of circumstances than from weakness of character), and the possibility of such an occurrence adds another reason to those mentioned in the first chapter, to the desirability of occasionally changing the rounds of the audit clerks. Imagination (under proper control) is another very desirable quality in a clerk, for without it, he is apt to become a mere machine, and consequently absolutely useless to the Auditor.

"THE AUDITOR'S POSITION. The position of the Auditor varies to a certain extent with the nature of his appointment, and it will therefore be well to consider some of the circumstances separately, under these varying conditions, before discussing these points that are common to all.

"THE AUDITOR TO A SOLE TRADER will, in almost every instance, receive his appointment from such sole trader in person; the appointment being—in the absence of stipulation to the contrary—for the period covered by the Profit and Loss Account, but renewable upon the same terms for each successive period, unless a contrary arrangement be made. The fee for the first audit is sometimes settled beforehand, but more usually left open until the time occupied has been ascertained, the fee for subsequent audits being usually arranged after the completion of the first audit.

"Naturally, the fee charged will be a matter of arrangement; but, in the event of no definite sum having been agreed upon, the Auditor would—in case of disagreement—be entitled to such sum as a jury would award, which would probably be the usual professional charges. There would be no especial limit to the responsibilities of an auditor to a sole trader : if he certify a set of accounts as correct any third party (e. g. a bank advancing money) relying upon his certificate, would probably have exactly the same right to expect the accounts to be accurate as though the audit had been performed in pursuit of their own instructions. This is a point that should not be lost sight of, as one is very apt to rely upon the unsupported word of one's own client. An Auditor might resign his office at any time, but it is doubtful whether he could then claim to be paid for the time occupied upon an uncompleted audit. On the other hand, the client might at any time discharge his auditor, but he would probably be held liable for the whole fee of the current period, if the audit had been actually commenced.

"THE AUDITOR TO A FIRM is usually appointed by the mutual agreement of the partners; but, occasionally, by the articles of partnership themselves, or by one particular partner. If appointed Auditor *to the firm*, he must, however, in either case, consider *each* partner as his client, and protect the interests of each accordingly. The same conditions as to term of agreement, responsibility, fees, and resignation, obtain to the auditorship of firms, as were mentioned in the previous paragraph; but it would seem that any one partner would have power to bind the firm as to the amount of the fees—except, perhaps, where the appointment lay in the hands of one partner, when the consent of such partner would probably be required. Probably no one partner could discharge an Auditor without the consent of all his co-partners.

"THE AUDITOR ON BEHALF OF CREDITORS.

"It not infrequently occurs that a retiring partner, who leaves a portion of his capital in the firm, or a creditor who makes an advance to a firm, stipulates that " Mr. So-and-so shall audit the accounts.', Unless the contrary intention be very clearly expressed, the Auditor so appointed would act on behalf of both the firm and the creditor. In such a case it is very desirable that the amount of the fee be arranged beforehand, and it would not be wise to leave it an open question as to who was to pay it. Under the circumstances the firm could not, of course, remove the Auditor without the consent of the creditor, but, unless there were a special provision to the contrary, the creditor could do so at any time, although, probably, he would be obliged to indemnify the firm against any extra expense occasioned by his so-doing.   The position of the Auditor, in such a case as this, closely resembles that of the Company Auditor, except that the creditor would be entitled to the fullest possible information, while it is sometimes a question as to whether shareholders have an equally extensive right.

"THE AUDITOR OF A COMPANY is appointed, in the case of a new company, by the directors, but he is subject to re-election at each successive annual general meeting, and at any such meeting the share-holders may (theoretically) if they so please, appoint another Auditor. Unless the renumeration of the Auditor be fixed at the time of his appointment, or by the Articles of the Association, he is entitled to such sum as the shareholders, in general meeting, may award him—and no more.   A casual vacancy has usually to be filled by an appointment at an extraordinary general meeting, but some articles of association give the directors power to fill a casual vacancy.   To a great extent it rests with the directors to decide how much information shall be supplied in the published accounts; but the Auditor must not lose sight of his indi-vidual responsibility, and he should never certify a Balance Sheet to be 'full' merely because he considers it to be as 'full' as he may think it expedient for it to be.   Rather let him, in such a case, certify the Balance Sheet, 'in his opinion, to be a fair Balance Sheet, and to suffic-iently disclose the financial position of the company.'   On the other hand, he should be particularly careful to guard against juggling with words, and so appearing to give a full certificate, when in reality he is 'making himself safe,' or 'hedging' behind a certificate which, when carefully analyzed (and only then) is found to be most qualified.   He must, in every case, be satisfied in his own mind that the accounts are correct, and fairly stated.

"OTHER CONDITIONS govern the appointments of Auditors under various general and special Acts of Parliament, but these may be readily gathered from a perusal of the particular Acts involved, and—as the differences are, for the most part, merely formal—need not now be entered into.

"THE LIABILITIES OF AUDITORS.   Turning now, again, to the general aspect of the question, it will be well to consider the extent of the Auditor's liability in connection with accounts that he has certified as being correct.

"The question appears to be capable of division under two heads: viz.

"(1) What is the actual extent of the Auditor's guarantee of accuracy?

"(2) What is his legal responsibility in case of an error being subsequently discovered in accounts that have been certified by him?

"TO MAKE THESE TWO POINTS SEPARATELY.

"THE EXTENT OF AN AUDITOR'S GUARANTEE. Unfortunately, this is a matter upon which the profession are by no means agreed; while, on the other hand, the cases that have been decided by the courts are so few, and the questions at issue actually so narrow, that sufficient precedents are not available to definitely settle the matter. At the same time, it is well to remember that, however desirable it may be to know exactly the bare extent of the legal responsibility, the real professional responsibility to clients ought always to be the ideal, and, further, an Auditor will be the worst of friends to his profession if he studiously exert himself to narrow the responsibilities, and so to dwarf the importance of his position.

"The responsibility involved in certifying a Balance Sheet to be absolutely correct is so great, so limitless, that many have preferred to discard all claim to such a position of certainty, and prefer merely to certify a Balance Sheet as being "in accordance with the books." Auditors, however, will hardly require to be reminded that an investigation which had been limited to the comparison of the Balance Sheet with the books would be, for every purpose, absolutely valueless. So obvious is this conclusion that no professional Auditor would ever think of confining his investigation to this particuler point, yet many experienced Auditors appear to be afraid to make any certification as to the result of such further investigation as they know to be essential. Such a state of affairs is unsatisfactory to the client and discreditable to the Auditor. Again, it is a very open question as to whether so unsatisfactory a certificate would ever have the effect of limiting the legal responsibility of the Auditor to the exact points certified. It is, at least, possible that the court would view the matter from a broader aspect, and consider that the man who had accepted the position of Auditor, to say nothing of the fees incident thereto, had also undertaken the responsibilities of that position, and that it would be disposed to form its own opinion as to the real extent of such responsibilities. Such indeed, appears to have been the view taken by Mr. Justice Sterling, in the case of *The Oxford Building Society.* It would appear, therefore, that the Auditor who does not consider his investigation has been sufficiently searching escapes no liability by issuing a carefully modified certificate: and, indeed, such a course is decidedly unmanly, somewhat dishonest and exceedingly childish. These are strong words, but not stronger than the circumstances appear to require.

"When addressing the Autumnal Meeting of the Institute of Chartered Accountants in 1888, Mr. Frederick Whinney, F. C. A., expressed himself as follows: "I know perfectly well that a proper Auditor must go further (than comparing the published accounts with the the books) and see that books themselves do correspond with facts," and this view appears to be endorsed by the legal decisions to be considered later on. As to how far it is possible for this standard to be carried into practice, there is perhaps some room for the elasticity of individual opinion, but the general statement is absolutely unassailable.

"In actual practice, however, the question naturally arises: How is the Auditor to ascertain the actual facts? To which it may be replied: In the same manner as a jury—*by sifting evidence.* The chief evidence is, of course, the books, (and it may be remarked, incidentally, that it is clearly the Auditor's duty to see that the accounts he certified, in addition to being correct, are in accordance with the books), but the books must not be considered the sole source of evidence; the fact that a statement appears in the books is *prima facie* evidence only, and must be verified, not only by internal cross-examination, but also by reliable and independent evidence.

"The result of such an examination will be that the Auditor has proved to himself that certain statements represent absolutely indisputable facts, and that certain other statements *in his opinion* appear to represent facts. Beyond this—not being omniscient—he cannot go, and should never attempt to go. Let him therefore certify that he has thoroughly examined the accounts, that they are in accordance with the books, and are in his opinion, correctly stated: he will then be occupying a logical, manly position—far more in keeping with the dignity of his profession than that afforded by the most skillful of word juggling.

"THE RESPONSIBILITY OF THE AUDITOR FOR ERRORS. Having now considered the practical extent of the Auditor's certification of correctness, let us consider what will be his liability in the event of his investigation having failed to detect errors or frauds.

"Having regard to the weighty responsibility resting upon the Auditor, and the enormous power—for good or evil—exercised by him, it is reassuring to find that there exists no single instance of a competent and conscientious Auditor having been held liable to reproduce moneys that have been lost to his clients by his inability to detect an error in the accounts he has certified.

"The decision of MR. JUSTICE STERLING, in *The Oxford Building Society* case, is perhaps one that more clearly affects the profession than any yet given. The head-note of this case reads as follows:

'Held that it was the duty of the Auditor in auditing the accounts of the company, not to confine himself to verifying the arithmetical accuracy of the balance sheet, but to enquire into its special accuracy and ascertain if it contained the particulars specified in the articles of association, and was properly drawn up to contain a true and accurate representation of the company's affairs.'

"That portion of the judgment which more particularly affects Auditors enforces the same doctrine in even more definite terms.

'In each of these years, L. (the Auditor) certified that the accounts were a true copy of those shown in the books of the company. That certificate would naturally be understood to mean that the books of the company showed (taking for example the certificate for the year 1879) that on the 30th April, 1879, the company was entitled to "moneys lent" to the amount of £29,515, 15s 0d. This was not in accordance with the fact; the accounts, in this respect did not truly represent the state of the company's affairs, and it was a breach of duty upon L's part to certify as he did with reference to them. The payment of the dividends, director's fees, and bonuses to the manager actually paid on those years appears to be the natural and immediate consequence of such breach of duty; and I hold L. liable for damages to the amount of the moneys so paid.'

"The futility of an Auditor attempting to escape his just responsibilities by a limitation of the scope of his certificate is here most forcibly demonstrated; there are, however two other points, which must not pass unnoticed.

"Firstly, there was no question, in this case, as to the accounts being false.   The matter in dispute was no moot question of depreciation or of apportionment between Capital and Revenue; the accounts were indisputably false, and it was not even suggested that the Auditor had done his best to verify their accuracy.   Had there been any possible doubt upon this score, and had the Auditor conscientiously attempted to perform his duties, it is not unreasonable to suppose that he would have received the benefit of any doubt that might have existed.

"Secondly, the immediate result of his neglect was a payment of dividends, directors' fees and bonus.   Had no such result taken place, it is by no means so certain that any liability would have accrued.   It would probably be considered a question open to argument, as to whether the failure of an Auditor to detect fraud was the direct cause of loss to his clients; so far as the money already stolen was concerned, it would appear that the cause cannot well be preceded by its effect, while it is not quite obvious that even subsequent frauds would be the direct result of the Auditor's neglect.

"The point is rather a nice one, and—as far as the author's knowledge is concerned—still undecided.

"Before dismissing this case altogether, it may be well to remark that L. was allowed the benefit of the Statute of Limitations; but—inasmuch as this point was not disputed by plaintiff's counsel, and was consequently not before the court—it does not follow that a like plea would avail upon another occasion.

"To sum up, then, it does not appear that the conscientious and capable Auditor, who has endeavored to conduct his audit upon the lines laid down, need feel the least apprehension as to the legal consequences arising either from a *bona fide* error of judgment, or from his inability to discover an exceptionally clever fraud.   On the other hand, it would doubtless be greatly to the advantage of all properly qualified Auditors if even more were expected from them, for there **might,** then, be some chance of scaring out of the field a **too numerous class of** so-called Auditors, whose extreme ignorance of the various elements of their profession is only equalled by their utter inability to appreciate the moral responsibility of their position.

"CONCLUSION. Nothing now remains but for the author to take leave of the indulgent reader, upon whose kindness he has already trespassed to considerable length.

"In dealing with a subject so new to literature, the author cannot but feel that the present contribution will be found, in many respects, insufficient to meet the wants so generally felt by the profession for a complete and standard work upon this most important branch of the Accountant's occupation:

* * * * * * * * * *

"Meanwhile the author feels that, if he has only called increased attention to the extreme difficulty and responsibility of an Auditor's position, his present labor will be by no means thrown away. Even at the present day the importance of a complete audit is by no means universally recognized, and that in spite of the pregnant words of the immortal Bard who—three hundred years ago—reminded us that

> ' Omission to do what is necessary
> Seals a commission to a blank danger,' "

THE END.

INDEX.

INDEX.

THE DEVELOPMENT OF
CONTEMPORARY ACCOUNTING THOUGHT

An Arno Press Collection

Baldwin, H[arry] G[len]. **Accounting for Value As Well as Original Cost** *and* Castenholz, William B. **A Solution to the Appreciation Problem.** 2 Vols. in 1. 1927/1931

Baxter, William. **Collected Papers on Accounting.** 1978

Brief, Richard P., Ed. **Selections from Encyclopaedia of Accounting, 1903.** 1978

Broaker, Frank and Richard M. Chapman. **The American Accountants' Manual.** 1897

Canning, John B. **The Economics of Accountancy.** 1929

Chatfield, Michael, Ed. **The English View of Accountant's Duties and Responsibilities.** 1978

Cole, William Morse. **The Fundamentals of Accounting.** 1921

Congress of Accountants. **Official Record of the Proceedings of the Congress of Accountants.** 1904

Cronhelm, F[rederick] W[illiam]. **Double Entry by Single.** 1818

Davidson, Sidney. **The Plant Accounting Regulations of the Federal Power Commission.** 1952

De Paula, F[rederic] R[udolf] M[ackley]. **Developments in Accounting.** 1948

Epstein, Marc Jay. **The Effect of Scientific Management on the Development of the Standard Cost System** (Doctoral Dissertation, University of Oregon, 1973). 1978

Esquerré, Paul-Joseph. **The Applied Theory of Accounts.** 1914

Fitzgerald, A[dolf] A[lexander]. **Current Accounting Trends.** 1952

Garner, S. Paul and Marilynn Hughes, Eds. **Readings on Accounting Development.** 1978

Haskins, Charles Waldo. **Business Education and Accountancy.** 1904

Hein, Leonard William. **The British Companies Acts and the Practice of Accountancy 1844-1962** (Doctoral Dissertation, University of California, Los Angeles, 1962). 1978

Hendriksen, Eldon S. **Capital Expenditures in the Steel Industry, 1900 to 1953** (Doctoral Dissertation, University of California, Berkeley, 1956). 1978

Holmes, William, Linda H. Kistler and Louis S. Corsini. **Three Centuries of Accounting in Massachusetts.** 1978

Horngren, Charles T. **Implications for Accountants of the Uses of Financial Statements by Security Analysts** (Doctoral Dissertation, University of Chicago, 1955). 1978

Horrigan, James O., Ed. **Financial Ratio Analysis—An Historical Perspective.** 1978

Jones, [Edward Thomas]. **Jones's English System of Book-keeping.** 1796

Lamden, Charles William. **The Securities and Exchange Commission** (Doctoral Dissertation, University of California, Berkeley, 1949). 1978

Langer, Russell Davis. **Accounting As A Variable in Mergers** (Doctoral Dissertation, University of California, Berkeley, 1976). 1978

Lewis, J. Slater. **The Commercial Organisation of Factories.** 1896

Littleton, A[nanias] C[harles] and B[asil] S. Yamey, Eds. **Studies in the History of Accounting.** 1956

Mair, John. **Book-keeping Moderniz'd.** 1793

Mann, Helen Scott. **Charles Ezra Sprague.** 1931

Marsh, C[hristopher] C[olumbus]. **The Theory and Practice of Bank Book-keeping.** 1856

Mitchell, William. **A New and Complete System of Book-keeping by an Improved Method of Double Entry.** 1796

Montgomery, Robert H. **Fifty Years of Accountancy.** 1939

Moonitz, Maurice. **The Entity Theory of Consolidated Statements.** 1951

Moonitz, Maurice, Ed. **Three Contributions to the Development of Accounting Thought.** 1978

Murray, David. **Chapters in the History of Bookkeeping, Accountancy & Commercial Arithmetic.** 1930

Nicholson, J[erome] Lee. **Cost Accounting.** 1913

Paton, William Andrew and Russell Alger Stevenson. **Principles of Accounting.** 1918

Pixley, Francis W[illiam]. **The Profession of a Chartered Accountant and Other Lectures.** 1897

Preinreich, Gabriel A. D. **The Nature of Dividends.** 1935

Previts, Gary John, Ed. **Early 20th Century Developments in American Accounting Thought.** 1978

Ronen, Joshua and George H. Sorter. **Relevant Financial Statements.** 1978

Shenkir, William G., Ed. **Carman G. Blough: His Professional Career and Accounting Thought.** 1978

Simpson, Kemper. **Economics for the Accountant.** 1921

Sneed, Florence R. **Parallelism in Two Disciplines.** (M.A. Thesis, University of Texas, Arlington, 1974). 1978

Sorter, George H. **The Boundaries of the Accounting Universe** (Doctoral Dissertation, University of Chicago, 1963). 1978

Storey, Reed K[arl]. **Matching Revenues with Costs** (Doctoral Dissertation, University of California, Berkeley, 1958). 1978

Sweeney, Henry W[hitcomb]. **Stabilized Accounting.** 1936

Van de Linde, Gérard. **Reminiscences.** 1917

Vatter, William J[oseph]. **The Fund Theory of Accounting and Its Implications for Financial Reports.** 1947

Walker, R. G. **Consolidated Statements.** 1978

Webster, Norman E., Comp. **The American Association of Public Accountants.** 1954

Wells, M. C., Ed. **American Engineers' Contributions to Cost Accounting.** 1978

Worthington, Beresford. **Professional Accountants.** 1895

Yamey, Basil S. **Essays on the History of Accounting.** 1978

Yamey, Basil S., Ed. **The Historical Development of Accounting.** 1978

Yang, J[u] M[ei]. **Goodwill and Other Intangibles.** 1927

Zeff, Stephen Addam. **A Critical Examination of the Orientation Postulate in Accounting, with Particular Attention to its Historical Development** (Doctoral Dissertation, University of Michigan, 1961). 1978

Zeff, Stephen A., Ed. **Selected Dickinson Lectures in Accounting.** 1978

DATE DUE			
3-21-88W			
2-23-00			